James Lee Purnell Jr.

Memories of
Struggles and Progress in a Segregated
Worcester County, Maryland

James Lee Purnell Jr.

Memories of
Struggles and Progress in a Segregated
Worcester County, Maryland

James L. Purnell Jr.
Kimberly A. Chase

ANCESTORYBOOK PUBLISHING
Fort Washington

2017

Copyright © 2017 James L. Purnell Jr. and Kimberly A. Chase.

All rights reserved. No part of the book may be reproduced or transmitted in any form or by any means, electronic or mechanical, including photocopying, recording or by any information storage or retrieval system, without the written permission of the authors or ANCESTORYBOOK Publishing, except for the inclusion of brief quotations in a review.

Publisher's Cataloging-in-Publication data

Names: Purnell, James L., author. | Chase, Kimberly A.
Title: James Lee Purnell Jr. : memories of struggles and progress in a segregated Worcester County, Maryland / James L. Purnell Jr. ; Kimberly A. Chase.
Description: Includes bibliographical references and index. | Fort Washington, MD : Ancestorybook Pub., 2017.
Identifiers: ISBN 978-09772822-7-2 (Hardcover) | 978-09772822-6-5 (pbk.) | 978-09772822-5-8 (ebook) | LCCN 2017951016
Subjects: LCSH Purnell, James Lee. | Businessmen--Worcester County (Md.)--Biography. | African Americans--Eastern Shore (Md. and Va.)--Biography. | Eastern Shore (Md. and Va.)--Biography. | Worcester County (Md.)--History. | African Americans--Segregation--Maryland--History. | African Americans--Eastern Shore (Md. and Va.)--History. | BISAC BIOGRAPHY & AUTOBIOGRAPHY / Personal Memoirs | BIOGRAPHY & AUTOBIOGRAPHY / Cultural Heritage
Classification: LCC F187.W7 P87 2017 | DDC 975.2/1--dc23

Cover Design by Kimberly A. Chase

First published in 2017 by ANCESTORYBOOK Publishing
Typeset in Palatino Linotype
Printed in the United States of America

To Mom & Dad
-J.L.P.

To the elders whose stories we tell
-K.A.C.

We know and consider that a nation is not born in a day. We know that large bodies move slowly . . . A battle lost or won is easily described, understood, and appreciated but the moral growth of a great nation requires reflection, as well as observation, to appreciate it.

-Frederick Douglass (1864)
"The Mission of the War"

Contents

	Preface	viii
I.	We Needed That Love to Survive	1
II.	We Didn't Miss a Beat	15
III.	Early Firsts	27
IV.	That Pretty Wife of Yours	31
V.	Where Were Y'all Been At?	35
VI.	After She Died, He Began to Live	43
VII.	Nigger, Get Off the Street!	49
VIII	Briddelltown	55
IX.	Camp Decatur	61
X.	Markers in God's Water	65
XI.	The Boom	67
XII.	I Ain't Superstitious	71
XIII.	Reasons	79
XIV.	Making History	87
XV.	Stagnant Progress in Our Schools	97
XVI.	The Downfall in Coming	103
XVII.	Advice	107
	List of Image Sources	111
	Index	113

Preface

I was on vacation in the Berlin/Ocean Pines/Ocean City area just over a year ago when my uncle and godfather, the subject of this autobiography, initially brought up this project. My interviews with him, whose content compose the bulk of this autobiography, came ten months later.

The elders of his community (the "icons", he called them) were gone. He found it hard to believe that he is now an elder in the Flower Street neighborhood, and he had a story to tell.

There is an astounding lack of literature on the black experience in Worcester County, Maryland, let alone told from an African-American point of view. The spate of histories about previously segregated locales that have been published have little to no input from people of color. There is little to no mention of black businesses and institutions.

The story of James Lee Purnell Jr.'s childhood is relatable to most African-Americans in the area of his time. Yet the course that his life took is unique for its place in the 275-plus year history of the county. The collection of stories within are a glimpse of black life in not just Berlin, but the surrounding area, transitioning from segregation to full civil rights. The turning points of his life are those of the county.

I want to acknowledge my husband, children, brother, and niece for accompanying me on my extra trips over to the Eastern Shore so that I could conduct interviews. I also want to thank my aunt and godmother Clemeth Purnell for her hospitality for the hours that we invaded her home.

I can honestly say that this was the easiest book that I've written to date, and I enjoyed every minute of it. I look forward to another project about my home away from home.

Kimberly A. Chase
8/9/2017

I

We Needed That Love to Survive

I was born in Worcester County, Maryland, here in Berlin, in a little town called Briddelltown, on July 26, 1937 to Hulda and James L. Purnell Sr., at the house down on Flower Street that we just demolished. I was raised there on a dairy farm that my mother and father owned.

I can say this with all sincerity, about not only my brothers, but my sisters. You can find that we are a close-knit family. We are very supportive of each other and that all comes from good home bringing up by our parents. We were taught to love each other and we try to live up to that. I look at some families today, especially brothers and sisters and how they get along. I can't understand why. I don't know how they can live like that.

In life, regardless of how good you try to make it, sometimes you have a stumbling block along the way. You have to learn to step over that stumbling block and life goes on. That's the way I've found it to be with us. I've learned in life that you cannot live a good, happy life with hatred, or have hatred for your own brothers and sisters, mother and father. It's a disaster and I can't live that way. Mom taught us not to live like that. She had no hatred, but she told you what was on her mind. Now that's where I come from.

Daddy called Mom Duke. Now where he got that from, God only knows. I never did learn where he got it. Her other nickname was Hilda. Hilda and Hulda got mixed up through the spelling some kind of way. I always heard Hilda Purnell, but then again, I heard the right pronunciation was Hulda Purnell. I don't know where the Duke came from. I'd like to find out, but we'll never know now. I know Dad called her Duke quite a bit.

Then sometimes he'd get serious and call *"Hilda."* It was *"Duke, Duke"* when she was cooking dinner or something. On Sunday morning, we'd have those yeast rolls Mom would make. One Sunday, Mom didn't make yeast rolls. She made flour bread and it was good too.

"Duke, where are the biscuits?"
Mom said, *"You're eating them."*
"I ain't talking about them. I'm talking about the other ones."
Mom said, *"I didn't make them this morning. I made a change."*
"Okay."

The only name I've ever heard her call him is James. That's the only thing I've known her to call him. I never heard Jim out her mouth. Mom never called me James and Dad never called me James, just Junior.

Gerald's got a nickname that Dad gave him, Beau. I know where that one came from. There was a black prize fighter called Beau Jack and Dad used to listen to him on the radio all the time. Dad said Gerald looked something like Beau Jack, so he nicknamed him Beau. He didn't have a nickname for Ben. Patricia had her nickname, Tisch. Hennie had hers. They started out calling her Henrietta and that didn't work right. That's the only other name we ever had for Hennie. Hennie accepted Henrietta before she accepted Hennie. She didn't like Hennie because it was her grandmom's name. Mom Hennie's reputation wasn't too good. Hennie had sense enough to know then. She was old enough to know that.

My brother Jock had a heart in his body of gold. He would do anything for you when he could. I find that my brother Osie's the same way. Jock was the oldest, Osie was next to him, and then there was Virginia, who some of the younger ones did not know. Then along came me, Edward, Tisch, Ben, Gerald, Gilbert, and of course Hennie and Bert behind them.

I have no memories of Edward because Edward was born right along after me. We both ended up with the same sickness, and I survived it and he didn't. That was pneumonia. I have never, ever . . . and I guess we never will see a picture of Edward. When they moved his grave, I was the one that dug it up. Gerald's the one that made the concrete vault that we put him in and moved it over there where Mom and Daddy are now. Mom helped to do that.

Now Gilbert . . . Dad always said he was gonna be the smartest one of the family. I wonder sometimes if he had lived, how smart was he going to be, based on what Dad said. I've heard Aunt Alice, Mom's sister, say that he was doing things at his age that you ordinarily wouldn't see a child that age do. He was trying to learn how to count without anybody telling him.

Gilbert was sort of Bert's complexion and, compared to Gerald, Ben, and myself, he had right nice-looking hair like the ones younger than us. I guess his hair was shaped up something like Bert's and Hennie's. When Gilbert left here, he was not two years old.

He swallowed a bean that came out of the garden. Well, it cut off his air passage. When I got home from school, Aunt Winifred was there. Dr. Nickels, our family doctor, was there, and he told them the only thing he knew to do was to try to get him to Temple University Hospital in Philadelphia, Pennsylvania.

Aunt Ella Mae's husband named Ari had an old Hudson. That thing would fly. So, he loaded them all up, Mom, Dad, Aunt Ella Mae, and Gilbert. Aunt Winifred stayed home with us. He had this white rag tied on his car somewhere and they said he was moving. Mom held him all the way, but said when they got around Dover, he was turning bluish-looking or something.

When he got to Philly, a cop pulled up behind Ari as he got ready to get out there at Temple University Hospital so he could get Mom and them in there. The cop wanted to talk to him. He told him, *"Man, I ain't got time to talk to you. Leave me alone. We got somebody here dying."*

I don't think the cop wanted to believe what he was saying, but he was telling the truth. So, once he got them situated, Ari came out and then he talked to the cop. The cop let him go and decided he was telling the truth.

When they brought Gilbert home from the hospital, they had his body all fixed up by a white undertaker uptown named Burbage. They brought him home, put him at the foot of the stairway on the side, and that's where he stayed. The funeral was held there in the house. I think it was Reverend Marks or Ballard who preached the funeral. Then they carried Gilbert to the cemetery to bury him.

Now, I would go to boy scout meetings. By the time I got back home, most of the time Mom,

Dad, Tisch, and them all had gone to bed. I had to go by that casket to go upstairs to the bedroom, and I would turn the light on, sometimes stop there, and look at him. I would always rub his hands and stuff, and I'd go on to bed. I'd go to sleep.

I talked to Aunt Ella Mae about it. She'd say, "Junior, you mean to tell me that ain't scared you, when you went to bed?"
I said, "Went on to bed and went to sleep. He can't bother me."
She said, "Well…".
I said, "You got people out in this street that'll hurt me, but he ain't bothering me."
She said, "Yeah, honey, you're right."

That's what Aunt Ella Mae would say. I can remember that very clearly. So that's the fine memories I have of Gilbert.

I had the opportunity to be around Virginia quite a bit, because Virginia and my cousin Viv were first cousins. Aunt Vic was Viv's mom and Dad was Virginia's dad, so they were very close. They went to school that way. They sang. Vivian could sing and Virginia could sing in school. Virginia was one of the first ones to win a scholarship out of Worcester High School. She was very smart.

She ended up going to the Philadelphia Apex School and being a beautician. That kind of hair grease and stuff they had, it's different now. Without a mask over her face to keep from inhaling it, back there then, she ended up with Tb and that's what she died from, Tb.

There's been a lot of sadness, which hits all families. You have to learn to accept it. I remember Gilbert. I couldn't remember Edward. The first one we lost after them was Virginia. Then along came Jock, and then after that was Hennie.

Those are things that hit your heart real hard, but you have to look up to which your help comes from and get strength and move on, because life has to go on. You go on carrying those memories with you as long as you live. That's what I'm gonna try to do for the rest of my life, acknowledge the memory of them for all the good that they have done, not only for me, but for their families as well.

My earliest memory I guess goes back to when I was about roughly four years old. I can remember Mom taking us to Frankford Camp. Back there in them days, one of the highlights of my life was getting to go to Frankford Camp and stay a whole week. Dad half the time didn't want us to go, because he wanted us to stay and work on the farm. He finally found out that when Mom told him we were going, she meant that. Tisch and I went, and then finally Gerald. He got to crying one time and Grandpop had to bring him back home.

Frankford Camp at that time had all outside toilets, and I ran around with cousins that lived up there. They said that I started a fight with Bill Beckett, Mom's sister's boy. When I'd done that, I wasn't even five years old and we were both the same age. He was taller than me and a little bit heavier, but I used to be halfway . . . a little mean though, back in them small days. I was mean. We got to tussling and going on. His brother Alex talks about it now. He said, "Bill said, 'You know what, if I didn't have my feathers, Junior would have killed me'." We never figured out what he meant by that.

Another early memory I had was when a white lady passed by that house where Mom and Dad lived. It was dirt road then. She was going down to the landfill, because they just opened it. The county opened that with promise of closing it in one year, but they lied to Daddy and they talked another woman out of selling her right-of-way through there. They got there and then they didn't want to close it. Anyhow, this white lady . . . her and another white lady, passed by that afternoon. I was out there, sitting to the step all the way out to the road, and I had an old comic book, Red Ryder and Little Beaver.

I was reading that. Let me tell you. Little Beaver was an Indian and he had a feather up on his head like this sticking up. Red Ryder was the cowboy. So, I would get that comic book, and I'd read it sometimes after I come home from school.

Mom wouldn't say nothing then if I hadn't done my homework. I could read it. I can remember that very clearly just like it was yesterday. That comic book was 10 cents. You can't beat 10 cents. If you bought a comic book now, it would cost you more than $2.00 to read it. That's what I read mostly, cowboy books.

I did have a few white friends when I was a boy. One lived across the field from Mom and Dad, right along there where that middle school is now. It's on the same property. Their last name was Baker. They worked for Harrison, who had one of the largest orchards on the East Coast. We'd go over there and play, and they'd come over to our house and play.

Farther down the road where they're building this new development with some townhouses going up now, there used to be a man named McCabe... Morris McCabe I think. We were very close friends of theirs.

There was another one of them around my age and his father owned the Berlin Milling Company where Dad spent all his labor. We were very close friends. So, we had a few white friends.

When I was old enough to go to school, I attended the one on Flower Street right down the road here from the first to the ninth grade. We walked to school with no bus transportation. We walked when it was raining or snowing. The weather was never too bad for us to stay home unless it was a strong hurricane.

I was lucky to be brought up in this community that we had. People cared for each other. There were times when we'd be in school and it rained so hard. A man by the name of Ernest Henry lived two doors or three doors from where we lived. He was a brick mason and he wouldn't be working, so he'd go to the school and pick us up, but he had a daughter there. He would pick us up and drop us off all along the road until he got to our house.

Then there was another man who happened to be my Uncle Elwood, my dad's brother. He would sometimes go out there and pick us up when it was raining or the weather was bad, and bring us home. Of course, at that time our mother wasn't driving. Dad was at work.

That's the only means of transportation we, not only myself, but other boys and girls that grew up with me in this community, had. That's the only way we had to get home. We walked from home out to Flower Street. There were no concrete or blacktop roads here. It was all dirt and mud.

I can remember back in the day, it must have been 1949, or maybe 1950. I was walking to school and Mom told me to look after Tisch because it was real muddy down through here. It was so bad that cars didn't go through. Tisch got stuck in the mud up over top of her rubber shoes that she had on. I walked off and left her and went on to school. A man across the road named Mr. Bob Dennis went out there and got Tisch. He got her out of the mud, got her in the house, cleaned her shoes up, and dried them off, and then saw that she got back home. When I got home, I got a whipping for running off a leaving my sister in the mud.

We as a group of boys and girls in this neighborhood, we were fortunate enough to stay together all the way through high school. One of the girls who walked with me back and forth was named Minnie Jarman.

Girl, 15, Fatally Burned At Home

BERLIN — A 15-year-old Negro girl burned to death at her home here when a kerosene stove exploded and ignited her clothing.

Dr. N. E. Sartorious, Sr., Worcester County deputy medical examiner, said Minnie L. Jarman suffered burns over her complete body, except for her feet. The doctor listed the death Friday as accidental.

According to the medical examiner the girl, a freshman at the Worcester County High School in Snow Hill, had come home from school and was lighting the stove when it exploded. She went through two rooms to her own bedroom and wrapped herself in a blanket. She was home alone at the time.

Her father, Robert J. Jarman, an employe at the Acme Poultry Co. here, and firemen arrived about 4:30 p.m. Mr. Jarman found his daughter's body. Fire and water damage to the house was extensive. No estimate of the loss was available.

Besides her father she is survived by her mother; two younger sisters, Clara Mae and Anna Margo Jarman and a brother, R. J. Jarman, Jr.

A funeral service will be held in St. Paul Methodist Church here at 2 p.m. tomorrow. Interment will be in Berlin's Evergreen cemetery.

Friends may call from 8 to 10 p.m. today at the home of Mrs. Carrie Fassett Spence of Flower St. here.

When I went home one night, I happened to look across the field and the house was on fire. I did not know she was inside. We found out she was in the house and found dead, but she did not die from the blaze. They said Minnie died from smoke inhalation. She was in the ninth grade when that happened, so that really put a setback on us as children growing up in this community. We happened to be around her age.

I graduated from the ninth grade at Flower Street and went to Worcester High School in Snow Hill. The high school was on Royal Street. In the meantime, they were building the new high school just below Newark, Maryland. They named it Worcester High School and all the ninth, tenth, eleventh, and twelfth grades from Berlin and the city of Pocomoke, we all came together.

About eighty-two of us went down in the tenth grade from all three schools. Eventually I would say the total population of that school would be something around 275 to 300, because you had other grades there, which were high school grades. Two years later, they opened the new school in Newark, which now houses the Board of Education complex. In 1955, I graduated from there.

We've had all kinds of acts of racism in this county against us as colored people. It's hard for black kids coming up in this world today in the state of Maryland, and especially in the community where I'm at, where they are today, to understand.

It starts in the school system, in elementary school. When we were going to school, we didn't have access to new books. The books we got for education, whether they be math, we called it arithmetic then, reading, English, or whatever, had been used by the white kids first. They were hand-me-downs from the white schools. When they got tired of them, the white schools got new books.

These books had pages torn out of them and the Board of Education sent them to us. I had a great love for history. I picked up this book on George Washington Carver and part of the pages were missing.

In our classroom, we'd see things written in those books like *"Nigger don't read this"*, *"Nigger"* this, *"Nigger"* that. And that's the kind of books we were accustomed to, but through it all, we did get an education. It should not be a surprise that Worcester County was one of the last counties in Maryland to integrate its schools or the last county in Maryland to recognize Martin Luther King's birthday.

It's been a rough, tough time, and a rough journey for those who came along with me, and some that came ahead of me as well, especially our parents. You had to have strong parents who did not give in. That's the only way they could survive, by not giving in.

Growing up in this community at a very young age there was a lot of love with the family and the neighbors who lived in it. We looked after each other. Back then, we needed that love to survive. If we didn't have that, we never would have survived.

II

We Didn't Miss a Beat

As I grew old enough to understand what a pig, a chicken, or a cow, or a duck was, it was the beginning of that farm. It never was called Purnell Farm. It was called Purnell Dairy Farm. A lot of other things came before that dairy farm did. There was a chicken house on that farm down there. Dad and his brother Uncle Elwood raised a large number of chickens, up in the thousands.

There was a poultry plant up in Berlin called Acme Poultry. They would buy the chickens from Dad, Uncle Elwood, and them. The catcher would come get them in the early morning or midday. They had a guy go in the chicken house, grab one of the chickens, and weigh it. Then, he would tell Dad how much he would get a pound. They don't do that now. Those chickens back then were weighing three and a half, four pounds, some of them five pounds. Dad was getting somewhere in the neighborhood of fifteen, eighteen, sometimes twenty cents a pound, or more. So, Dad raised chickens for quite some time.

Then along came the hogs on the farm. Those hogs were only there for survival as a form of food. Ham, scrapple, sausage, spareribs, you name it, whatever came out of that hog, was there, and we ate it.

A few men who lived out here in the neighborhood of Flower Street slaughtered them. They were good friends of Dad and his father as well. One of them was named Mr. Snipe. His right name was John Briddell. He went to our church and sang on the choir. There was Mr. Henry Derrickson who lived out Flower Street. His house is still out there in front of where the Multipurpose Building is now. Another man was named Mr. Bill Best. He lived right down the road across the railroad tracks. Then we had one named Joe Foster. Joe Foster was the man that made cooking lard. He was hanging around because he was going with our Aunt Ella Mae at the time. Her and Aunt Hattie were the ones who made the scrapple, sausage, and all.

Dad would kill his hog one day, and the next day his dad would kill his. Next day, a man back in the field back here would kill his. They all used the same man. The old men would get their old bullet rifles, short-handed bullet rifles. They came walking down the road, and they'd get to our house around 5 o'clock in the morning most times. I'd be waiting when they got there. Dad would get up, go on downstairs, go out there, and start lighting the fires outside. I'd be out there with him, lighting the fires and getting the water hot enough. Mixing lime in the hot water caused the hair to come off the pig easy.

When getting ready for the lard, you'd put the cracklings in the lard press after you coat them in grease, you'd turn it, and you'd squeeze all the grease out of it. Mom and them put it in containers and that would turn right white. They called it lard grease or cooking grease. That's how Mom and them cooked by anyway.

The sausage was made by Dad's sister Ella Mae and his Aunt Hattie. Dad's aunt lived to be 103. She cooked her breakfast and dinner every day. Now Aunt Ella Mae and her would make the scrapple, make the sausage, and nobody around here that could make it like them. That's the truth. They stood by their making of sausage and scrapple. Then they would cut tenderloin out of there. Boy, that was good steak. When you'd taste that stuff, it'd be tenderloin.

After that, Daddy decided to go in the dairy business. When Dad went in the dairy business and that chicken business at the same time, that was unknown for a black man to do that around here. He went and bought a young calf, and he had numerous young calves that he sold, but he kept this one. We trained her and everything, and she came of age to give milk. So, he started selling it. Dad finally took her to a farm over here, had her bred with another bull, and then she had a calf. Dad also went and bought two cows up to Willards, brought them home, and put them in the cow pasture. One of them was mean. She would kick you and everything. The pasture was where Cousin Viv lives now. All that back there was pasture. Dad owned quite a bit of land.

We had those cows trained so that I could put three of them side by side with a chain run through their collars, put three more behind them, put three more behind them, three more behind them, and they'd follow these three cows. At that time, it was a dirt road. They would come down that dirt road on the side so the cars wouldn't hit them. I didn't have to lead them. Sometimes I'd walk ahead of them. I just had a little light switch to touch them if they got out of that line. Very seldom they did that. I could put down that gate when I got there. I didn't have to take that collar and pull them over. They'd take their time, wiggle their ears and stuff, and go on in that pasture.

All of them would eat and then about a certain time of day, they'd be standing out there waiting for me, all twelve of them. Now most times when I was going to school, I'd get down there around four o'clock and bring them home. Most times, they'd follow right to the barn right behind the house. I'd put down the gate. They'd go on in. Then I'd change my clothes, get out there, and start milking cows. At times, Dad would get home and he would help finish up. Gerald wasn't quite big enough then, but later on Gerald got big enough to milk cows too.

We got them milked and then in the morning around 4 o'clock, Dad and I would be out delivering milk in all kinds of weather. We had some people who lived on the camps, what they called migrant workers, who came from down in North Carolina. They were all black people and they ended up staying up here to work in the chicken plant. They were able to run a tab with Dad.

Dad had one side of the street and I had one side of the street. I delivered milk on the north side. On Sundays, we'd collect money. Then we'd carry it home, set it out on the table, and count it. I'd pick up money on my side. I wouldn't let anybody have credit, but he would. There was a woman named Ms. Jean Knight who was part Indian and had pretty hair.

She told me, *"James Jr., I tell you I don't have no money today, but come Friday, I be able to give you my money."*
I said, *"No, Ma'am. I gotta have the money for the milk now."*
"No, I . . . I don't have it, I told you."
She went to get Dad, *"Mr. Jim?"*
Daddy goes, *"Yes, Ma'am?"*
"It be alright if I get a get a quart of milk until Friday?"
Dad said, *"Yeah. Junior, go ahead and give it to her."*

To tell you how much she thought of that man, she ended up leaving here and going down to Tampa, Florida. She had a daughter who went to school with me named Shirley Knight who had cat eyes, and her son too. Anyhow, she left here and went down to Tampa and she owed Daddy some money for milk. She came back here a few years ago, looking for Mr. Jim. Dad been dead ten years when she came back here.

She said, *"I had just heard some sad news and Ms. Rebecca told me that Mr. Jim passed away some ten years ago."*
I said, *"Yeah. He did."*
She had tears in her eyes right then, *"Mr. Jim left here and I owed him for 3 quarts of milk."*
I said, *"It wasn't but 15 cents a quart."*
She said, *"Will you take it?"*
I said, *"No, I won't take it. I didn't charge you that. I didn't give you credit. He did."*

Shirley and Carlton, her children, were standing over there. She said, *"Well how will I ever repay him?"* I said, *"Well, if you get to Heaven, you can pay him there, or you can carry it down to the cemetery and put it on the grave."* That's just what I told her. She told me I was crazy. She was a very nice lady though. So, we gave a lot of credit and we had some white people who bought milk over there in town.

Mom made butter from the cream from that milk. We started out with all the cream. Mom would get a quart jar and get all us children, and we'd beat on it and it would turn to butter. Finally, she ended up getting a butter churn. I don't know what happened to it, but you'd crank it and it would make butter. On Friday nights, Mom would have as high as fifteen or twenty cakes of butter. They'd be about that big around and she had a mold to put the flower in the middle of them.

The man who ran the A & P store uptown bought all her butter and put it on the counter and he resold it. Man, them people up there buying that butter went crazy over that country butter. That whole block probably didn't cost over 75 cents and you couldn't buy it now for $3.00 a pound. Sometimes he'd have people baking cakes out St. Paul. They'd get milk from him and all that, but he had a great dairy business.

We also had rabbits and grew quite a few of them. Daddy got them for us. We used to go hunting rabbits, but we didn't eat these because they were pets. One day, we were making rabbit cages. Gerald was holding this board and I had this saw. The saw slipped and hit his thumb. I had cut some of it off.

We both ran into the house together to tell Mom. She just jumped in the car and away we went. Mom got us to the black doctor named Dr. Salley. When Mom got up there, the doctor saw the only thing for him to work with was skin. He took the scissors and clipped that skin and his thumb fell off the rest of the way. The doctor bandaged it. So, Gerald came home with part of his thumb gone.

This nub and everything was all bandaged up. He kept a big bandage around it until it was all healed.

There came a time on the farm that Daddy took sick. It was more or less his nerves than anything else. I was twelve years old and I had to run the dairy farm by myself. Mom ran the chicken farm by herself. I think Tisch was old enough to help her with straining milk and putting it in quart jars and stuff. Mom would ride with me, and I would drive the car at twelve years old. Sometimes she would drive, and we'd go deliver the milk.

I went back home. I had to do the same old chores and get the cows to the cow pasture, come home and get ready to go to school, and be at school by 8:30. We used to go to school half a day, so by 12:30 we'd be out of school. I'd get back home and have the same routine. By then, Daddy had bought a tractor. That was for me to plow the land up and plant the corn, the hay, or whatever. I did all that and at the same time, had to garden. We all had a garden of things for us to eat. So, the whole time Daddy was sick, we didn't miss a beat. Between Mom and I, we kept things going. Eventually, he was able to get back to work, which was a good thing.

His illness was discovered by a German doctor by the name of Dr. Robertson, who was a family doctor, and our family doctor as well. He examined Daddy who didn't want to accept he was sick. He wanted to keep right on working. Then finally his boss man that owned the business had to come and to let him know that they weren't going to let him come to work because his health wasn't just right. The good thing about it, Dad still got paid every two weeks. You have some jobs that don't do that now. You have some of them that do, but a lot of them don't. So, he got paid every two weeks. He got 800 and some dollars. That was good money back there then in '49.

Dad was in car accident right at Flower Street with his own car. He was on his way to work with his father and his brother. He picked them up right down the road and went across the bridge. It was foggy and a man named Mr. Quillen, who lived out there where all them Brittinghams are now, sold fish and stuff. He was out that morning for some reason. It was foggy as I don't know what, and Daddy was on his way to work around 7 o'clock up to the Berlin Milling Company and they went together. It seemed like Old Man Quillen had pulled out in front of Daddy or something, and he hit him. Old Man wrecked his car, a 1934 Ford, somewhat.

Dad came home and had a cut right over his eye. He walked home from where the accident was, down the road 'til he got back in our house. Finally, the boss man sent his car out there and sent one of them employees to take Daddy, Uncle Elwood, and Pop Lee to the hospital to get them checked out . . . the father, and two sons . . . and they carried them.

They sent Dad back with this patch over his eye and that stayed like that for about two weeks, then they took it off. They didn't put no stitches in it, because it was too close to his eyeball. When they took it off, you couldn't tell where he had been cut.

One day, Dad came home from work and the Board of Health was there. They said that the reason why they were there was because of a report that his cows were dirty and the milk wasn't clean. Well, that didn't stand up because he washed those cows just like Mom would wash her young children, every day. He'd hose them down with soap and water, and wash them off.

What happened was there was a black man in this community who was jealous of him. This man had a business too. He was a landscaper and he reported that, but he was buying the milk off of Dad. On Saturdays he'd buy 2 quarts, 1 quart every day, and two on Sunday. Most of Dad's customers bought a quart of milk every day. Well come to find out, the Board of Health did all it could to investigate and it gave the cows a clean bill of health. So, he kept right along. We never did miss a beat anyway.

This is what got Daddy out of the dairy business. With all of the health regulations coming down from up high, from the federal government, it would have costs him thousands and thousands of dollars to do what they wanted and keep that business going. He would have to put in a septic stall, a place for a cow to walk in and lock her neck in there, and he'd have to put what they call kickers on the legs. He'd have to buy his own milker to milk the cow.

Dad was a believer, and so was this old white man here, that you should not put them on cows, because if they overdo it, they cause the cows' udders that hold the milk to go dry. That's one of the reasons he didn't do it, but they tried to make that mandatory, but it wasn't.

There are some things about milk the average person may not know. A cow can eat a certain food and she will produce more milk than she will with other foods. A cow can eat a wild onion and you can't use the milk. That wild onion taste comes out in the milk. So, we would have to throw that milk away.

Pasteurization lasted one year and they did away with that too. It went through something like thinning the milk out, adding water, and all that, and the milk became more of a bluish-white than it was white. There was a special machine to do that. Milk lost its taste.

When they came down with all these regulations, Dad said he just wasn't going to do it, not for thousands and thousands of dollars. The highest people paid for a quart of milk then was twenty cents. Sometimes the cream would be that far down, and you had a lot of people down at Flower Street on them old camps and stuff were taking that cream off and they'd make flour bread with it. They had a lot of use for a quart of milk, more than drinking it. So that's why Dad got out of the dairy business, because of the regulations.

III

Early Firsts

My entertainment was mostly around sports, playing baseball. That grew up in me because of my dad. He was a baseball player. My friend that lived right down the road, across from Mom, used to be a baseball player. I grew up as a baseball player and we formed a team here. In fact, I played with a team from Snow Hill. Then we had two teams in Berlin. We finally ended up using one called the Berlin Eagles and I played on that team. We traveled up to Bridgeton, New Jersey and all that. We had scouts come here and look at us play, and the only thing that kept us out of the minors or the major league was our age. I was too old.

We had one guy who lived across the field who died. He was a pitcher. My cousin Oliver down the road was a pitcher. I was a catcher and outfielder. I used to go out and watch Daddy when he was playing in his later years. I used to watch him play out Flower Street with some of his friends down here, and I picked it up. The reason I became a catcher was probably when I was up to Buckingham High School. Back then it was all white. I had been learning how to catch behind the plate, and this boy, their catcher, got hurt. Daddy had a friend named Howard Scott that worked with him up to the feed mill and he knew I could catch. So, that white boy got hurt and Howard Scott said, "Jim, can you put your son back there?" Dad said, "Yes, if he'll go."

That was the first game I ever caught. I went back there and I caught behind the plate. Dad and I would ride up there on bikes and ride back. After all that happened, years later, I thought it was strange. They didn't do anything about it. I thought maybe they would go and have a race riot or something. No, those boys were around my age, some of them were older, but they accepted it I guess.

I was the first black to ever work in a laundry around here. It was the Sunshine Laundry, right there where the Food Lion is now. Ralph Davis ran the Sunshine Laundry. I was in the eleventh grade when I went there and applied for a job. Before I could walk out the door, he said, "*When can you start work?*"

At that time, I was extracting, that means pulling the clothes out of the big washer, putting them over in the extractor. You'd see them spinning around and around and around, spinning the water out of them, and then you'd put them in the dryer. Then they'd come out of that. A lot of the work we did were sheets and pillowcases from Salisbury Hospital in the peninsular region. Atlantic General Hospital wasn't even thought about then.

SUNSHINE LAUNDRY
Says
Now It's...

3 *for free*

IF WE MISS A BUTTON!

- Yes, if we return a shirt with a button missing we'll launder FREE that shirt plus two more!

- And here at Sunshine your Dry-Cleaning receives the same careful attention!

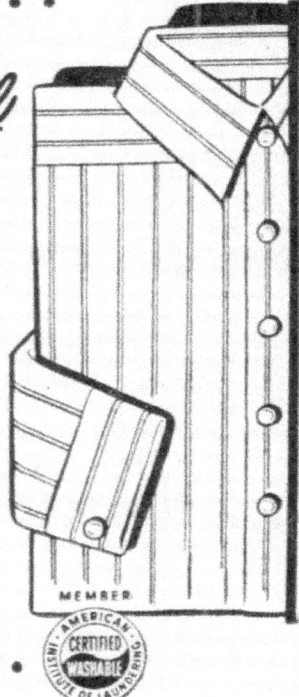

Phone 2-1111

Later on, I moved on up the ladder and became a head washer. $1.85 an hour was what the head washer was getting then. That's what I ended up getting. Later on, my brother Benny worked there. By that time, there were some more blacks, men and women, working there then, but I was the first one to ever work there. He trusted me and gave me the job, and I stayed there until I got out of school.

IV

That Pretty Wife of Yours

Bud Britt, they called him, was Aunt Alice's husband. His right name was John Brittingham. That was Osie's wife Delores's daddy. He and Daddy were just like brothers. They worked together during their young years before they even got married. They worked together up here to Harrison's nursery. They even worked together in Jersey. A lot of people don't know that. Daddy worked in Glassboro, New Jersey for a man that owned these peach orchards and stuff. They'd stay and come back on weekends.

I'd say he and Dad were together almost all the time. When Dad got a job up at Berlin Milling Company, up there where he retired from, Dad's father was already there. Then Dad's brother Uncle Elwood was there. Then, so was Aunt Alice's husband Bud.

It came around wartime, World War II, and they started drafting men for the Army. If you had two, or three, or four kids, you got something they called a deferral, or something like that. They wouldn't draft you, but if you didn't have any kids, you could almost consider yourself going in the Army. The man that lived on other side of Mom, one of them Johnsons, he left here and went into World War II at 42 years old. He ended up cooking potatoes and stuff in the Army. So, they were drafting and calling men in to go get examined for the Army and all that. Bud evidently had received this letter to go get examined.

He began to get a little worried about going in the Army. So, the black men that worked up in

Berlin Milling Company with Daddy, about three or four of them, used to tease him, *"Man, when you go to the Army, man, we going get that pretty wife of yours,"* this, that, and the other. It went on and on, and finally, it got to him.

Bud drove a truck of all feeds. Dad didn't drive. He mostly ran the mill. Dad said that come lunchtime, Bud would go out there, lay on the ground, and pretend he was working underneath this truck, like he was greasing. Bud wasn't doing anything, just laying up there. His mind was getting bad. His mind was beginning to deteriorate. So, that went on and the next thing we know, his mind snapped. He hit Aunt Alice across the head, I think with a pitcher of water.

Eventually, they sent him to Crownsville, right off Route 50 down there by Annapolis. That's where they used to send crazy people who lost their minds. He stayed there about three or four months. Aunt Alice and all of them used to go see him. I didn't.

When Bud came home, and way before he went to the hospital, I used to ride with him all the time. Dad would let me ride with him, of course quite naturally, because that was his best buddy. They were closer than Dad's brother Elwood was to him. That's how close they were. So, when he came home from the hospital, I'll never forget, he had this '37 Chevrolet with the gear in the floor. I used to get in and ride with him different places. He used to drive up to Frankford and everywhere. All of a sudden, his mind started snapping again, and they sent him back to Crownsville.

He came back home again in May. I was in seventh grade or eighth grade. The school out here to Flower Street, that was torn down, it had what you used to call May Day, wrapping the flag pole, and I participated in that. Aunt Alice drove over to the school because Mom wasn't driving then. I went over to Uncle Britt and Aunt Alice's house. He and I walked from his house across the field down to where the school was.

The people who attended were from everywhere. We went there and stayed all day long. He seemed like he was doing alright. The next day, he snapped again. When they carried him away from here that time, he didn't come back anymore. They had him tied down too.

Uncle Britt died in the late '40s. He and Aunt Alice had only been in that house, not a year, when he passed away. I went to his funeral. He had a gold tooth. He was buried with that gold tooth in his mouth. He had a scar up on his head where someone claimed he'd been struck with a chain.

V

Where Were Y'all Been At?

A few of Mom's uncles, stayed down here with us at Mom and Dad's house sometimes. Uncle Harv was down here more than any of them. He'd come down from Pennsylvania, *"I gotta come down and spend a few days with Hulda."* We called her Hilda. They called her Hulda. That was her right name.

He'd come down to spend some time with her, and then he'd go on to Frankford Camp. Tisch and I would go and stay until Camp was over. Then, I'd stay an extra week with Grandmom and Grandpop, and come back home. School would start the week after that.

My Grandpop John McCray always had a liking for children. When we got out of school for the summer, he would come down and pick us up. Our first stop would be to the tent out on the Campground. Grandpop named the tent "Baby John" after Mom's brother. After those two Sundays were over at Camp, we'd go back and stay at their house until it was time for me to go back to school. I'd come home. I didn't want to come home then.

When I stayed up there with them, he'd go working at Eagle Poultry as a handyman. Jack Udell was the owner, and they had some Germans up there then working in the poultry plant. We'd go up there to the Millsboro Dairy which had cartons of chocolate milk. They'd send them down with Grandpop in the back of his car. We gave the German prisoners chocolate milk to drink.

And sometimes on Friday night, he'd let me go with my cousins, George and Ben Beckett. They are Alex's brothers, but much older, and they had their driver's licenses. We'd go to the Ball or John M. Clayton Theaters up in Millsboro. One of them would carry us and the other would pick us up on Friday or Saturday night. Sometimes they'd come pick us up, and we'd have our girlfriends standing out there with us. We called them our girlfriends. They were supposed to be girlfriends, but they were a bit more girlfriends than a piece of paper. We were something. You couldn't tell us nothing.

When he was a young man, Grandpop came down here to Berlin. He was working down here when they built this highway going into Snow Hill and Pocomoke. He got a job working doing that and he worked at the basket factory uptown. The house he lived in is still out here to Flower Street. The woman that he boarded with was Miss Elkie Henry. It was her mother who owned the house then.

I know because she taught me in school. She didn't only teach me. She taught Daddy. Miss Henry started teaching when she was 15 years old. Back then you got a certificate to teach and she got it from Bowie State College, or somewhere like that. I think she taught every one of my siblings. She might not have got Bert or Hennie, but she got the rest of us boys and Tisch. Miss Henry taught Daddy and some people older than Daddy. That's how I found out when Grandpop stayed here in Berlin.

Grandpop went back to Frankford and met this woman they called Bertha. Grandmom's right name was Sallie Bertha Tyre. After they married, he brought his daughter Lib to their house. Grandmom raised her along with their three girls: Mom, Aunt Alice, and Aunt Annie. Aunt Lib was older. Aunt Bashie was older and her mother was a Showell. Of course, Aunt Bashie always stayed with her mother.

Grandmom was somewhat like Grandpop, but she was a little sterner than he was. Grandmom was very nice and could cook. Now, you take all of her daughters. Every last one of them were good cooks. She was about the same height as Mom. Mom favored her more than the rest of her sisters did. When I first saw Grandmom and was old enough to know who I was looking at, I thought she was white. When I knew Grandmom, her hair was just as snow white as it could be. She had medium length white hair. I saw her twin brother, Uncle Cyrus, and he did have red hair.

If Grandmom told you to do something, don't drag around and take your time. If you're to do it, then you do it. She had a little temper in her too. I never forget the time that Jock was old enough to drive. He had a driver's license and I was staying there. Grandpop let Jock have the car, but I had to go with him. I guess Grandpop thought that if I went with them, they'd come right back. Well, Cousin Bert wanted to go to Millsboro to see this guy named Johnny Steele. He was a nice-looking guy and that's the one Bert called herself liking. He had forty-eleven other women. We stopped at Millsboro to see him, and then go on all along with her.

Jock brought the car back in the yard and went on upstairs. He was getting ready to go to somewhere. It was about 8 o'clock that night and Jock had to work the next day. They kept asking,

"Where you been at?" Jock wouldn't say and Cousin Bert wouldn't say.

So, Grandmom came to me, "Junior?"
"Yes, Ma'am."
"Where were y'all been at? Where were y'all been at?"
I said, "Up in Millsboro."
"Huh?"
"Millsboro." I never did tell them about the guy.
She said, "Well, what you do in Millsboro?"
I said, "We were up in Millsboro. I don't know what the person name was. We were up in Millsboro."

Bert came downstairs, "Junior, Junior." She went on, laid me out, and was gonna hit me with something. Grandmom stopped her right in her tracks. She took that flyswatter and wore Bert's behind out with it. I never will forget that as long as I live. Mind you, Bert was almost a grown woman then. She was ironing some clothes when Bert did that. She threw the iron at her. Grandmom was a woman of her word. When she said something, she meant it.

I can remember when she got sick. We went visiting and Dad went too. I could hear all these rattles in her throat when she was breathing in.

We got home that night and Mom said, *"Your Grandmom ain't gonna be there much longer. I doubt if she makes it through the night."*
I said, *"Why Mom?"*
She said, *"She has death rattles."*

"What you mean 'death rattles'?"
Then she explained to me what they were.

Well, the next morning about 5:30, quarter to 6:00, Aunt Alice came down in her car and told her,
"Yeah, Mom died."
Mom said, "I told y'all."
So, Aunt Alice said, "Hulda, what time you going up to Mom's?"
She said, "I don't know yet. I got some clothes I got to put out to wash and put on the line. Gotta do this, gotta do that, then I'll be ready."

Ms. Dollie Shockley lived next door and when Mom told her about it, she said, "And you still working?" Mom told Ms. Shockley, "Look, Mom's dead. Ain't no need in me try and rush and kill myself." Mom kept her own good time. She went up there, but she didn't rush. She took her own good time going up there. Finally, she went up there, put all her children in the car, and carried us up there. They mostly left her in charge of everything. Then about five days later, they had her funeral up there. I know she didn't live to be 68 years old. Grandpop lived to be older than that.

They raised my brother Jock and my cousin Bert. Jock didn't live with us and Bert didn't live with Aunt Alice for many reasons. One was tradition. They were born in and grew up in that household. When Mom got married and moved here, Jock was living in Philadelphia with some of his relatives on his father's side, the Harmons and all. Jock was there for a period of time and then he came back home to Frankford to Grandpop and Grandmom McCray's house. A lot of people for a long time thought that Jock and Bert were brother and sister. When Cousin Bert went to New Jersey, it wasn't long before Jock went behind her. I've never known him to stay in Mom and Dad's house down there but maybe once or twice in my young days. I know that when Jock went in the Army, he came down here to Mom and Dad's. After that, Jock stayed in Frankford up until he got sick and his time of death.

I used to stay with Mom's uncle Eben Tyre, too. His hair looked just like white folks'. He was married, but he didn't have any kids of his own. He raised some of his wife's kids. They had a woman who was a schoolteacher who boarded there with them. I know Alex remembers her. We talk about her sometimes. Alex was trying to find a picture of her when we were talking about her once before. Uncle Eb had a well on his farm. This woman would get up every morning before she went to school and dip water out that cold well in the winter time. She would wash her face, hands, and everything in cold water. She would not heat water on a stove. She had some of the most beautiful skin you've ever seen.

Uncle Eb was the last of her uncles to die, and he was in his 90s. I can remember that just like it was yesterday. He was up in a Smyrna nursing home.

That Sunday morning, Mom and Aunt Alice decided they wanted to go up and visit him, and I drove. We walked in. Uncle Eb was looking at us as if he didn't know any of us. He kept looking straight at Mom, but he never did call her name. Mom said, *"You know who I am. You know who that is. That's Alice. That's Alice and this is your buddy Junior."* We went to see him that Sunday. He died on Tuesday, I believe.

At one time, he was a pretty wealthy man. He owned quite a bit of land when he died. Aunt Lib's son Bill Beckett ended up with the land. He sold it in building lots, except for what he left for Wilson, himself and his wife.

VI

After She Died, He Began to Live

Dad's father, Lee Purnell, was a very nice, gentle man. Pop Lee, as we called him, was quiet, but he'd sing a little bit. He smoked a pipe until around the time he left here. He smoked Prince Albert smoking tobacco. Pop Lee lived to be about 71 or 72.

He loved to be around his grandchildren, as well as his own children. Pop Lee had a horse. He went a bought me a saddle to ride it. I rode it on Sundays along with Aunt Vic's son, Tommy.

Pop Lee loved to hunt during rabbit season. He was a big rabbit hunter and got me rabbit hunting. Pop Lee bought me a gun and Mom Hennie didn't want me to have it, but I ended up with it anyway. The reason why she didn't want me to have it is because he took his money and bought it. She didn't want him to spend money on nothing.

If Pop Lee would see some of his grandchildren, he'd give them a quarter. Back then, that was a lot of money, and she didn't like that. She didn't like to see him giving his money away. When he got paid, she would take all his money, give him what she wanted him to have for spending money, and stick the rest of it down in her bosom. She was very close-fisted.

He may have had some money in the bank, but not much. Them old folks then didn't believe in keeping money in the bank, on account of that Great Depression.

Pop Lee didn't have many fingers. On one hand, he only had two fingers and a nub. On the other hand there was one finger and a nub, I believe it was. They got cut off at that Berlin Milling Company where he, Uncle Elwood and Daddy worked. He would accumulate money from the insurance company when he got some of his fingers got cut off. Pop Lee ended up getting a lot of money, something like $1900.00. It wouldn't be considered much now, not even a drop in the bucket, but back then it was good money. Good Lord, you were a rich man then. He was still able to work on the job after that, and then he retired on his own.

His wife Hennie was a lot different from him. Mom Hennie was born Hennie Mary Gray. She would go to church quite regularly sometimes, but her beliefs were different than any ordinary woman's that I've known. Even her three sisters were a lot different in demeanor than she was. She was domineering.

I'll never forget, my sister Hennie wanted her name changed one time. They wanted to talk about Henrietta, but Dad wouldn't let it happen. The reason why was because my sister Bertha was named after Mom's mother and Hennie was named after Dad's mother. Hennie didn't like that name, but she never changed it. Anyhow, she got over it.

When we talk about her, it's always *"That Mom Hennie . . . that Mom Hennie . . . that Mom Hennie . . . Mom Hennie was something . . .".* She'd go out in these handmade dresses that look like they hung unevenly. She had one old faithful hat she'd would wear all the time. When she fixed herself up, she wasn't a bad looking woman.

She had some very stylish sisters. They were just as sweet as they could be. Aunt Lizzie and Aunt Ella lived in Philly. Lizzie's husband died and we come to find out she was running the undertaker down here. She was spry. She'd have her rouge on and all that stuff. She'd come down here and would be stepping in those high heels. Aunt Ella was the same way. Madge was too, but not Mom Hennie. She was set in her ways and you couldn't get her out of them.

Mom Hennie was overbearing and she tried to tell her mom, dad, sons and daughters how to run their family life. She tried to tell Dad, but Mom will tell you if she were here today, she broke that up. Mom told Daddy, *"You don't live down there. You live here."* When they first got married, he bought that house down there and I think he paid something like $600 or $700. Daddy would get paid and his mom would hold on to his money. Mom and Dad wouldn't have any extra money.

Mom got in contact with her sister-in-law, Uncle Elwood's wife, and she found out that Mom Hennie was doing Uncle Elwood the same way. She said, *"Clara, I'm going down there and I'm going to straighten this mess out today."* She grabbed Tisch and she walked down the road. When she left Mom Hennie and Pop Lee's house, she had Daddy's bank book and what little bit of cash he had saved up there in the house. Mom made Dad carry her uptown later on and put the bank account in his name and her name. It stayed like that until they both went away from here.

Mom told Clara, *"You better go on down there and get your money and bank book."*
Aunt Clara said, *"Well, I don't want to have to tangle with…"*.
Mom said, *"You have to."*
Aunt Clara was scared of Mom Hennie, but Mom told her she wasn't scared of her.

Her brother's son Arthur Gray would drink beer quite a bit, and he hung out with Aunt Winifred. He and Aunt Winifred were first cousins. They were big time buddies too. He would go down to Mom Hennie's. She would cut him off at the door, *"You can come on in here, but you ain't going to bring that beer in here. You can come on in here, but you ain't gonna…"* do this or that.

She had ducks in their yard. You'd see hens and guineas. She'd walk right past them. She'd cook them. Mom Hennie made good dumplings and stuff. As long as she had a chicken on the table, I'd eat it. If it was anything like a possum running across the road, not me. She'd cook them.

Dad, Pop Lee, and I used to build rabbit traps. We'd set them out there in the woods, catch rabbits, and kill them. A lot of people ate rabbits down here until a few years ago. I don't want one now. Anyhow Dad had caught a possum in one of those traps. If you caught a possum, once you got that possum out and set that trap again, a rabbit wouldn't go in there anymore. You'd have to line it with apple skins and onions. Dad let the possum go. He was down at his parent's house one night talking to his Dad about this possum. Mom Hennie jumped up from that table like someone had stuck a pin in her, *"You done what?! Let that possum go? You know you should have brought that possum to me! I would have…"*.
Dad said, *"Well I'mma kill it. I'm gonna kill it and I'm gonna cook it."*

That's when I found out she'd been cooking possum all the time. I never ate possum and didn't eat squirrel. She loved squirrel down there.

Mom Hennie lived to be about 67 years old. When she died, Mom, Aunt Winifred, and Aunt Clara got ready to clean up the house. She didn't have a dirty house, but they wanted to paper one room in there. Mom Hennie had that antique wallpaper. They started tearing off this and tearing off that, and the money came tumbling out. They found close to $5,000 hidden in the walls. Pop Lee ended up with quite a bit of money.

After she died, Pop Lee began to live. He put a new roof on the house. He bought himself a television. At that time, it was the biggest one down in this area. He loved to watch boxing on there. We only had two channels. Sometimes if something was going on that people from the community wanted to see, they'd go to Pop Lee's to watch television.

My cousin Cat Mae stayed with Pop Lee, especially after Mom Hennie died. Because she watched over his father, Dad gave her a piece of land back there so she could build a house. That house is still back there now.

VII

Nigger, Get Off the Street!

There was a time that blacks were not allowed to stand on the streets in the Town of Berlin. Blacks were not allowed to even go into town unless you went to spend your money, and then we had to get out of there. Don't stand on the corner, please. They'd want to lock you up.

They had one of the filthiest bathrooms. That was the only one for blacks that they had. The door wasn't even halfway on it. Right behind where the town hall is now there used to be a firehouse. Across from that firehouse there was a bathroom that wasn't fitting for a dog to go in, and I didn't go in it. A lot of us didn't.

We were not allowed to even go and eat with the whites uptown. They didn't want us near them, because we were labeled. There was a restaurant in town called Rayne's, right there at the fork in the road. It's still there. It's integrated now, but I still won't go in it today. Blacks were not allowed. At that time, Red Star Bus Line ran through here, going south and north. You could catch it to go to Philly or wherever. You went in there, bought your ticket, and came right back out. If you had luggage, you still came right back on out. You couldn't stay in there. That stayed that way, I guess until close to the seventies. I knew a couple of black women who were in there, and men, who halfway refused to come out and the restaurant called the police on them.

I have yet, to this very moment, to step my foot inside that place and I don't intend to. The food may be fine. The hospitality may be fine, but I just don't care to go in there. As young boys, we'd ride our bicycles uptown. One time, we went in there to buy Coca-Cola. That was one of our favorite cold drinks. They wouldn't serve us, inside or outside. So, that's one of the reasons.

They had some people from Dutch country around here one time, and I still wouldn't go in there. Some on my committee were people out in Dutch country, very supportive, and they didn't like the idea of the way we were being treated as citizens. You weren't treated as first class citizens. There were dogs that they treated better than they wanted to treat us.

One Friday evening, Dad carried us uptown. We had to park on the street across from where Donaway Furniture is now. At that time, it was a tractor place named Von Davis's. Dad dealt with this man, so he parked his car over on the street across from there. Mom came out from the A & P grocery store, and then she went down to Joe Holland's Shoe Store with Tisch. That was on that corner of Main Street. I got out the car and I walked up there by myself. Mom, Tisch, and I walked in. She was getting these shoes for Tisch. Finally, she got the pair of shoes that she wanted and Mom went to pay for them.

Tisch and I walked outside the shoe store, went to the left, and were standing on the side of the building. Along came this police officer named Noah Hudson. Dad called him Nowie. He had his blackjack in his hand. I wasn't standing exactly close to Tisch. I guess I was a few feet from her. He hollered at her, *"Nigger, get off the street!"*

Of course, Tisch didn't know what was going on. She was only about six or seven years old at the time. I guess Tisch didn't pay much attention to him. She didn't move. The second time he said it, he hit her in the stomach with his blackjack. I took off running and told Dad. I might have told Mom first, and then went right out of the store and told Dad about it. So, Dad came walking up there. I showed him the police officer and he knew him. Dad asked him, *"What did you hit my daughter for?"*

Noah Hudson did an about face on the story then, "Jim, I didn't know that was your daughter...," this, that, and the other. Dad let him know right then that something was going to be done about it that night. Back then, black folks didn't say that to a white person. You had to mean it and know what you were talking about if you said it.

Dad worked for a group of men that were actually very helpful to their black employees, including Dad's father, his brother Elwood, and others. They were very nice to those men. Dad got in contact with them and told them what happened. That Sunday morning, Dad was milking his cows and here come these two police officers to the house, Noah Hudson and Elmer Shockley. He was the Chief. They came to ask Dad to not proceed with the complaint regarding Tisch.

Dad's name changed from "Jim" to "Mr. Purnell" when he wouldn't give in. Thank God, he didn't give in. Come Monday morning around 10:30, that guy had no job. They went to the mayor of the Town of Berlin, and Noah Hudson was let go. Noah begged and begged and begged to Dad, but he wouldn't give in. That was back in mid-forties.

I can remember, about two years in a row, going to a Halloween parade in town at night. They ran me and my friends out of town back across the highway. They didn't want us over there. For the next Halloween parade, we went and got a hammer and broke up a whole lot of bricks. When we came up on Branch Street, which was Maryland Avenue then, and we piled them up. They were so far away from town and out before we got to the dual highway. That was our ammunition. So, they ran us out of town again. When we got to that pile of bricks, they stopped, but we tore them up. If they could prove exactly who did it, we probably would have gotten in trouble with white folks, but they couldn't prove it. I imagine some of them were too sore to even try to find us, because we lit them up with them bricks.

When I was going to the movies at the Globe Theater, which is used as a restaurant now, they put the blacks up in the loft. The whites sat downstairs. They did that, time after time, and those whites who sat down below paid a penalty. We ornery, devilish boys had our way of getting our point across, dumping waters of all sorts down on their heads. We'd throw anything . . . sodas and peanuts. We'd sit along the back and then lean over to look at them. The Chief of Police would come up in the loft and look. Nobody had done a thing. We paid him no mind. No sooner than he'd get down the steps, we'd do it again.

We had some people who lived out on Flower Street who were from North Carolina. They came up here to work in the chicken plant and they wore gumboots that came way up. When they get done with work, they'd have feathers all over them. They'd go up in the theater, rub them feathers up in their hands, and spray them out. The white folks would look up and those feathers would be flying over top of their heads. They paid a price for making us sit upstairs.

Today, our kids growing up in this society don't realize what price we paid so they could walk uptown on Berlin streets. They don't understand what price we paid so they could sit down to eat a meal alongside a white person. They don't know what price was paid so they could go to the movies and sit downstairs instead of upstairs.

VIII

Briddelltown

There was a time when Flower Street stopped at the bridge. The road we lived on was called a rural route. In the nineties, it was changed so Flower Street would go all the way over to Seahawk Road. I can remember walking while white people drove down this road. Some of them devilish boys would call us niggers.

Way out behind our house there was a water hole. In the winter time, the water would freeze just enough where you could ice skate on it. People would come all the way across town and up Flower Street to it. Now I didn't skate on it too much because I knew I wasn't much of an ice skater. Playing after school, the boys would do it then, but it was a thin piece of ice that wasn't very thick. Mom stopped us from going. She was scared that if it got warm, the ice would melt and we'd fall through. That water hole sometimes had over ten feet of water. My sister Hennie fell through the ice once. I wasn't out there when that happened. It was cold. That much I know.

Mrs. Louise Henry, the woman who owned the Henry Hotel on the southern end of Ocean City, lived on our road. Her husband had passed away. She'd rent rooms to blacks and seasonal workers. Another black family owns the hotel now, but the original cookware, cooking stove, and iron beds are still there.

There were a few folks in the neighborhood who were memorable for the wrong reasons. There was a white man who used to come to our house to visit Daddy all the time named Josh McCabe. He was a dirty-looking man. He called himself Daddy's buddy. He'd sit in there, especially in the cold weather, and get to talking. He'd start cutting up, *"Black son of a b____! You black son of a b____ . . .".* Out the door he went. Dad made him get out of there. He'd do alright until he got to talking about and hollering S.O.B., black S.O.B., and all that stuff.

Josh McCabe was riding his bicycle one night. It was pitch black dark almost and he couldn't see. A couple of guys, I guess they were about eighteen or twenty years old, came jogging down the road. They smacked him in the face, knocked him off his bicycle, and kept running. You could hear him hollering, *"Hey, I'll get you, you black son of a b____! You black son of a b____, I'll get you!"*

There was a house painter in the neighborhood named Dave Hudson. He was a nice-looking man who had nice hair. He ended up being what you call "the community drunk." He lived right down the road. It had been said one time he used to try to go with Mom's sister, Aunt Alice. That was before he started drinking.

Dave Hudson would drink rubbing alcohol. He used to sniff that Sterno heat that was used to heat baby's milk back then. Most of all, he would drink wine. He would get drunk and come down this road cussing every word as he walked from that bridge down to his house.

He lived with his grandmother Martha Hudson, a short lady who smoked a pipe. She was a very religious woman. If Dad or someone didn't give her a ride, she'd walked to church every Sunday and back home.

Dave would have a spell, go a whole week and a half, and wouldn't drink a lick. He did all Dad's painting, the barn and the house. He painted that house I don't know how many times during the time I was living there. Sometimes he'd come by, borrow money off of Dad, and not pay him back. Then Dad would sometimes get him to work it out.

Dave would come down the road sometimes just as buck-naked as he came into this world. Next to where Pop Lee lived, there was Ike Jarmon's house. Dave would get right along there, he would cut loose, start cussing, just as drunk, and didn't have a stitch of clothes on.

Another man who lived down here named Jess Briddell had a few horses. Some of the men in this neighborhood wanted to break Dave from cussing, running around down here naked, and all. Jess had a horse whip and would crack it. Dad and them got out there, and Dave went out through them briars stark naked, a-hollering and hooping, jumping just like a rabbit. Them briars were tearing him up. When Dave came out on the road, he was somewhere before you get to my house. He kept going. Jess Briddell sat there with that whip, cracking his behind and tearing it up.

They couldn't stop him from drinking. Dave Hudson went to jail probably 30 times. He might have gone more than that. He'd go there sometimes and the longest he'd stay was a week. They'd release him. Then some of them white guys would get him out, and Dave would go do their painting. He'd go right back in jail again. That was his life. Sometimes he'd get all dressed up just as sharp, had his hair combed pretty. Come Monday morning, he was back on the job again, cussing and drinking.

At the old house that used to be right beside Mom and Dad's, they made beer and wine. I think that's where Dave Hudson was killed. Two people were killed over there. They found this man laying out there in the yard. They found him underneath the walnut tree and maple tree over there. There were all kinds of people, white and black, going up in that house and buying that homebrewed stuff.

The guy that rode the bicycle, Eddie Johnson, had a woman named Fanny Mae who lived there with him. Tommy Johnson and Charlie Johnson were there too. One of their mom's friends, Goldie Hood, came down here from Millsboro, Delaware. She was a real light complexion woman and had long pretty hair. They say she was part Indian. Mom knew her way before she came down here to Berlin. She'd come over to Mom's house all the time to sit and talk with her.

Goldie Hood lived in that house with the Johnsons. Sometimes her family would come down here, her sister, father, and all. They'd get to fighting. You'd see some fights. Them old Indians would come out there and get to fighting like I don't know what.

IX

Camp Decatur

When I was in the fourth grade, I had the opportunity to see and play with German prisoners. Everybody can't say that. At the end of World War II, there was a German POW camp across from where Stephen Decatur High School is now, just on the other side of Seahawk Road. We could see it from our house.

Before the camp in Berlin opened in 1945, there was another German POW camp over in Somerset County. Worcester County farmers and businessmen were short on labor because of the war, so they asked the government to build one here. Hundreds of Germans were brought here.

Harrison Nurseries owned the biggest portion of land on that side of the highway. It owned apple and peach orchards. The Germans came here and they used them to work along with the Bohemians. We used to call them Bohemians then, but they came from the Bahamas. They came over here and worked, picking peaches, apples, and things of that nature. Some of those Germans worked under Dad at the milling company.

On Sunday, Dad and I would ride down to that German prison camp and go inside. I would play baseball with them, not knowing what was going to take place later. A few weeks after that, I developed these little bumps on me. We found out they were German measles, one the worst types of measles you can get.

The bumps were all around my eyes. Tisch caught the measles from me. We were quarantined in the house in the back room. We had no natural light whatsoever for over two weeks because it would have damaged our eyesight. Mom and Dad put these quilts up to the windows to keep the light from coming in.

We could come out of that room maybe once or twice a day. Mom would go in there and feed us what little bit we'd eat and everything. After about four weeks, our homework was brought to us. We would do our homework. Eventually, the doctors lifted the quarantine. Not long after that, I ended up having to get glasses, but Tisch didn't.

Some of those Germans attempted to escape by building a boat, putting two motors in it, and gassing it up to go back to Germany. It was hidden down here behind the racetrack where the casino is now, behind a lot of brush and debris.

They snuck out from the prison camp and stole whatever material they needed to build this boat. They stole the metal from Phillips Canning Company and got the boat built. I understand it had two Chevrolet motors which were stolen. Back then, those were 44 or 45 engines. They had numerous 50-

gallon barrels or drums. Everything they had back there was stolen. Nobody noticed anything.

Those Germans got that thing running, but by the time they decided to make their move, they got caught. That's what stopped the boat from setting sail towards Germany. I saw it because we would ride our bicycles and go crabbing down there. After the boat was found, it was there for public view.

I guess they could put twenty-five to thirty people on that boat or ship. There was space for them to sleep and everything. It took them a while to build, because you could tell it was more than one person's idea. I never did learn what happened to that ship. It was cut up for scrap metal, but I don't know what was done with it.

That was part of the history in this community. Very few people living here now realize that there was a POW camp there. I tell that story to a lot of people here and they frown their faces in disbelief. I think that German prison camp is a story that deserved to be told separately.

X

Markers in God's Water

If you leave the town of Berlin and go to other parts of Maryland or to northern Delaware, it's hard for those people to believe when you start telling these true stories. Here we are sitting right next to Ocean City, one of the largest resorts in this great United States of America. Back then, blacks were not even allowed to go there and eat. We could go down and make beds, clean up behind them nasty people, but you were not allowed to go there and eat.

In Ocean City, there were two joints on the southern end of the island back then. Both were owned by white men who rented them to black men to run. There was a dance hall called Grand Terrace. Duke Ellington, Cab Calloway, and all the bigtime musicians performed at it. The city wouldn't let them stay in the Ocean City motels. They had to go elsewhere. Sometimes they were able to advertise to blacks in West Ocean City who would house them. We couldn't stay in those motels or condos. No, we better not be caught there.

There were Colored Excursions in Ocean City. The summer season would be over after Labor Day and most of the tourists who came down would be leaving that boardwalk for the final time then. They didn't want us there during the summer.

Come the Colored Excursions, the businesses on the boardwalk would begin to close down. Blacks could only go on that boardwalk after they closed down for Labor Day. Of course, the boardwalk didn't extend as far then as it does now. It stopped around 14th Street. They had a Maryland Day, a Delaware Day, and a Virginia Day for black people to come out to that ocean.

The white people did not even want to mingle with us in the ocean. Starting at 14th or 15th Street around Harrison Hall, they had something like wire markers stretched out from the beach out into God's water. Not to the ocean, but out into the ocean. That meant that we as black people could only swim north of that wire. We could not swim south of that wire, because that's where the white people were.

They didn't want to be in the water with blacks, but what stopped that water from flowing to and fro? If we're black and sitting on the north side, and they're white and sitting on the south side, when that current came in, and went back out, it passed us first. They had so much hatred in their hearts that they would go to some of the most foolish extremes to not be around black people. It was stupid. It was one of the stupidest thing in the world. That lasted a long time. Once the integration process began taking place, it started to fade away.

XI

The Boom

*I*n 1974 or '75, I went to trade school in Laurel, Maryland. That's where I took my training. It was furnished by the Whirlpool Corporation that builds washers, dryers, and refrigerators. I went, stayed there about three weeks, came home on the weekends, and ended up passing the test to be an air conditioner technician.

I was able to tear a refrigerator down until all its parts were spread all across the floor, put it back together, and make it freeze or cool. Then I was able to do the same thing with an air conditioner, which is somewhat different. I ended up becoming an air conditioning technician. I did a lot of repair work with those window air conditioners.

There was a furniture company by the name of Coastal Furnishings in Ocean City. I was down there doing some air conditioning work for them. They had a guy who installed draperies and had his own drapery business in Salisbury, but he stayed home that day. After I got done doing the air conditioning work, an owner came to me and said, *"Jim, how about helping me install them draperies?"* I didn't know anything about installing draperies, but I jumped right in with him and started helping him out.

When my wife and I went to Hawaii, that was the first time I'd seen those long vertical blinds. No one had ever installed them around here. When we came back from vacation, I ended up going to trade school in Hazleton, Pennsylvania. I mastered installations in two days' time, and then came home.

I started my drapery business around the time that the condo boom began in Ocean City. All those piles of condos were popping up here, there, and everywhere. There was a need for professional drapery installers who knew what they were doing, because people were paying top dollar for their material, and they didn't want it put up any kind of way. I didn't go in with a hammer driving nails in walls. It had to be done professionally, and I was taught professionally. I began to venture out on my own through Coastal Furnishings.

After one year, I ended up in Long Island, New York installing draperies, because of my professionalism. It showed in Ocean City. People who owned condos down here came from Long Island and Boston, Massachusetts. I would do their work and they'd say, *"Would you mind coming to our home and doing ours?"* If the price was right, I'd go. The man had a huge office. I did that and part of his house. I ended up in Washington, DC, down by where the zoo is. I did a whole lot of those houses all along that street.

Cleanness helped to sell my business. When I came off of that ladder, or whatever I was doing, when I walked out, that floor was just as clean as when I went in there. I didn't leave anything on the floor and took all my trash. I didn't scar any walls. If the walls were damaged, then the job would have been done for free.

It got to the point that it was just too much for one man. I ended hiring a guy named Gene Pennywell, then my nephew Terrence, and the boy across the street. It went on and on, then my nephews G.J. and Ant worked with me, and I paid them. I'd finish up and they would clean up. They'd take up all the boxes, the stuff all in the floor, and carry them out to the dumpster. People fell in love with Osie's grandson Dameion. Every time he turned around, they were tipping him $20. I just stayed busy. I could work sometimes until twelve or 1 o'clock in the morning.

In a period of ten years or more, based on business in the Ocean City condos and all those places, I probably did thousands of installations. At one point, I was doing five and six condos a day. We were really moving. We had to be good to move fast and do it right. I was blessed because not one job was I ever called back on. Not one.

I used to always hum to myself while I worked. One day, one of my white customers looked at me and asked me why. I said, *"Well I'mma tell you the truth. It makes the work go better."* She said, *"You got a point there. Well, let me ask you something. Why don't you use your ladder more often? All you're doing is ruining your back."*

I'm a short man. I'd be reaching up over my head. I had a little, short ladder and I didn't use it for tall curtains on pins and everything. I often talk about it now. She was 100% right. I pulled my back right out of place almost and that's why I have problems with it now. My back is what caused me to retire from the drapery business. It got to the point when we were putting rods together, I'd have to sit right down in the floor. I couldn't reach up over my head too much. So, finally I decided to let it go.

I often told them that I wished they'd kept it going, because that was a business that had already been established and had a reputation. All they had to do was keep it going. I had the tools they needed. I went with air guns. We didn't have to drill any holes. Those new condos were concrete. Those things would go right in the ceiling. I had all those tools and they could have kept right on and had three or four men working for them. I get calls every now and then from former customers wanting to know if I'm still installing draperies, because they never forget a good job. I got a lot of tips in it too, I must say.

XII

I Ain't Superstitious

My cousin Oliver Purnell was awarded a bus driver contract by the Board of Education and Ben Nelson, who was the Supervisor of Transportation. Oliver bought his bus, Number 34, off of a black guy named Britt Haney. It was new. He sold it to Oliver because this white lady who lived uptown had died and left Haney a big inheritance of money, an old antique Buick, and some land. Haney said he was done with the bus and wasn't going to drive anymore. He was done, so Oliver bought it.

The next thing I know, Oliver had a stroke and it paralyzed his left side. The next morning, I took over the bus driving for him, and his wife paid me. Finally, the Board of Education said he wasn't going to be able to function anymore as a driver. They'd have to sell his contract and Oliver would have to sell the bus. So, that's what they did. They came over and asked me if I'd be interested in taking the contract and the bus. I said, *"Sure."* That's how I got started back in 1976, and I've been a school bus contractor ever since.

When I started back then, probably about 90% or 92% of the drivers in the county were black, mostly men. There were two black women, Helen Dennis down in Pocomoke and Ms. Zula Waters down in Snow Hill. It might have been three. I know of those two. There was a white woman who retired last year who was the longest tenured driver in the state of Maryland. She had 62 years of service and started around the time I graduated. We had another black guy named Upshur Coard who started around her time, but he retired before her. He was a short guy who lived on Germantown Road and drove Bus 44.

In 1988, I bought another new bus to replace the one I bought from Oliver. In 1995, I bought another one. I already had Bus 34. When I ordered the new bus, the man in charge wanted to know what bus number to put on it. He told me I was going to have to keep the second bus and let the old bus for a spare bus. That was fine, because that's more money for me.

I said, *"I need a number to go on the bus I'm buying, so they can put it on there and bring it up here."*
"Alright Mr. Purnell, we'll have it ready before school starts."
I said, *"Okay."*

So, I waited for that number, and I waited, and I waited. The bus was being built down in High Point, North Carolina. One day, I called my Supervisor of Transportation. He was one of them high society rednecks. He wouldn't talk to me. He had a driver trainer who grew up in this area with us named Scotty.

Scotty called me one day and said, *"Jim."*
I said, *"What?"*
"I got the number for that bus."
"Yeah," I said, *"What's the number 'cause I gotta call it in to High Point so they can put it on the bus so they can get her up here?"*
He said, *"Bus 13."*
"Okay. Thank you."
He said, *"Did you hear what I said?"*
"What? What'd you say?"
He said, *"Bus 13."*
"Okay. Thank you."

I found out later that our Supervisor of Transportation was right along with him when he made the call.

So, about ten minutes later, the supervisor called me, *"Jim?"*
I said, *"What?"*
"This guy gave you 13."
I said, *"Yeah. I told him thank you. I done called down to High Point and told him to put 13 on that bus."*
"You did?"
I said, *"Yeah."*
"You not…"
I said, *"No, I ain't superstitious. Ever since I learned how to count, when I always got to 12, the next number was 13. So, I didn't stop. No, I ain't superstitious."*
"Man, you got a lot of nerve."
I said, *"You had nerve enough to give it to me, didn't you? You shouldn't have given it to me then. You had

the nerve enough to give it to me, so I had nerve enough to take it."

The news was all over town and all over the county bus association for a while, *"Jim Purnell got 13. Man, he's got a lot of nerve to put 13 on that bus."* He couldn't believe I took that 13. It's just a number. Put it on that bus and let's go. So, when I bought the next new bus, they asked me, *"Mr. Purnell, are you changing your bus number?"* I said, *"No, I ain't changing it. Don't y'all bother that number. Leave it alone."*

We had a state bus convention over in Ocean City. I'm the President of the Bus Association, and when he introduced me, he said, *"The man who is not superstitious. The man who does not fear 13."*

When I got up there, I said, "You didn't have to introduce me that way. All you had to do was go ahead and introduce me. I'd do what I am supposed to do and sit down. You're talking about 13. Thirteen ain't nothing but a number."
He said, "Man, I understand you had a lot of nerve."
I said, "Nerve for what?"
"To put 13 on that bus and drive it across the bridge and all that."
I said, "I've drove it across there and it wasn't 13. What's the difference?"

So, it didn't bother me none. That's how I ended up with Bus 13.

It's been a great experience during the forty-one years that I've driven a school bus, traveling many miles safely with no tragedies or accidents at all. There have been close calls, not of my doing, but I was able to avoid them up to this very present time. I can say that I've been blessed, considering the kinds of weather that I've traveled in. The rate of speed that I travel is not always slow. Everybody knows that.

I'm slowing down now. It's all due to age. Soon and very soon, I think I'll be putting the steering wheel down on that bus, hanging up that part of my life, hopefully moving on, but not doing a whole lot of hard work. It wasn't hard work. It's been easy work. I'm going a little while longer to see how things go, and then I'll make my decision. I don't plan on driving a whole lot longer though.

A friend of mine from Pocomoke retired at age 84 from driving a bus. He sat on the Board of Directors. Every once in a while, I'd run into him and say, *"Harrison, how are things going?"* He said, *"Jim, the worst thing I ever done is retire."* *"Why?"*
He said, *"I spend all my money to the doctor and the drug store. You know what? During the time that I was a bus contractor in my eighty-four years, I only went to the doctor three times."* One of them times was to get his teeth cleaned. Isn't that something?

It's been a wonderful, joy of a time driving a school bus. I say that because all those miles were not just around here, day in and day out. Anyone who drives a school bus has to love kids, because they get on your nerves quickly. I've witnessed and come through all of that.

When you're talking about kids, things have changed. We live in a part of the country down here, where there are a lot of transfers from out of the big cities. There are different elements of people. We have to deal with different, unwanted things that come along with them.

In these last few years there are drugs, which I don't see a whole lot of, and profanity. These kids have no respect for anyone. Now some do, not all of them, but some of them. They have no respect for the people that they are around, not only bus drivers, but teachers and people in general. They say anything. They think the world owes them everything. It's to the point now that boys will tell us to *"go F yourself"* and all that. That's what's helped a lot of these drivers to decide to retire now.

Years ago, you didn't hear that kind of language. It's not accepted now, but what bothers me is the school system's failure to come up with a stiff punishment to deal with it. It'll pat them on the hand and say don't do it again. That doesn't mean anything.

We have cameras on our buses that are supposed to be tracking the students. If they were, they would cut out this mess with these kids. Them cameras are in there to catch the bus driver if he does something wrong. That's all.

I have traveled to Asheville, North Carolina with the ROTC, my wife Clem, and I took some other kids along with me. We'd stay there a whole week. These kids had the pleasure of crossing the Smoky Mountains in a school bus and visit the Black Hills. We went there maybe six or seven years straight.

I've driven my bus across Morgantown, West Virginia, as high as 5,000 feet up with those ROTC kids, different groups, but the same organization. We'd stayed with them a whole week, and they experienced things that they probably wouldn't have if they stayed home. I didn't see it, but one night one of them came face to face with a bear. There's a lot of bears around the Morgantown area of West Virginia. You see signs all along the road.

A journalism class and a business class have gone to New York City every year and stayed four days and I've taken them. They've gone to different types of shows, gone to Madison Square Garden, and have eaten dinner at one of the expensive restaurants across the street. I didn't have to pay. My meal was free.

I've had the opportunity to travel as far as Memphis, Tennessee with the AAU Boys Basketball team, and we stayed there a whole week. This was a group of young black boys around the age of twelve. We stayed across from Graceland. When they got through playing one afternoon, Clem and I took it upon ourselves to carry my little niece Taylor, those boys, their coaches, and the people that came with them to the Lorraine Hotel. They had the opportunity to visit the site where King lost his life, the room where he laid until they picked him up, the garbage truck, the car of the man that supposedly shot him, and one of King's Cadillacs that he used for traveling.

Those kids were delighted that they got the chance to see that. They may have lived the rest of their lives hearing about Martin Luther King, but not visited where this tragedy took place. So those kids today, long out of school, often ask, "*Mr. Jimmy, when are you going back to Memphis?*" I said, "*Well, if I do, it won't be in no school bus. I hope not anyway.*"

XIII

Reasons

Mom was a gutsy, little woman. She is one of the reasons that I got involved in politics. We had been talking about the landfill behind our house for a long time, because of the odor that came from it. In the summertime at night, it was almost unbearable to sleep with your windows up because there was no air conditioning. Hardly anyone down in this neighborhood had air conditioners. The smell of that landfill is what got me and other people involved.

There was so much garbage in that landfill because the heavily populated Town of Ocean City used it as their dumping ground. They had one in the Ocean City area, but it closed down. They came over here after that and dumped tons and tons of their trash there daily. They would not cover it then. They could just dump it and go on about their business.

I came over one night to Mom and Dad's house and got my start right there in her kitchen. Mom and Gabe Purnell said, *"Junior, we want to talk to you about being the chairman of the committee to close the landfill."* I said, *"I don't know if I want to be the chairman or not."* They said, *"Yeah, you're the one."* So, I let them know in a couple of days whether I was the one or not. Then we took off. Mom was right along there with us. Two other women, who lived a bit down the road, jumped on the bandwagon when they saw Mom was with us. It was called the Briddelltown Improvement Committee and our first challenge was to close the landfill behind our house.

I talked to the president of the Worcester County branch of the NAACP and pulled supportive people from the community to work with us as a group. We sued the county and they dragged their feet, as the old folks say. The lawsuit ended up in Washington, D.C. and with the Board of Health in Baltimore City. Finally, Worcester County gave in because of pressure from the Maryland Board of Health. The landfill had to cover the garbage to keep the odor down.

In the meantime, the Board of Health discovered that our water system was being polluted by that landfill. A lot of people didn't realize that back in that landfill there's more than thirty-five to forty feet of garbage underground. That's where the water table is, and that's why some people's water was contaminated, especially on that side of the ditch. That's one of the reasons that we were able to get that landfill closed. Because of that, we got a sanitary water system. We no longer have separate wells, because the water comes from a water system that's furnished by the Town of Berlin that now comes this way.

It took us three and a half to four years to get that landfill closed. We accomplished what we intended to do. Once we won that lawsuit, Worcester County had to abide by the rules and regulations that were set forth. I was told we would never win that lawsuit, but bottom line, we were victorious.

Many people don't realize that Worcester County was the last county in the state Maryland to recognize Martin Luther King's birthday. It was one of the most segregated places to live back then. I got involved in the NAACP because of things that I witnessed as a young child and as a young adult. For many years nothing changed.

Route 113 runs north and south through the Town of Berlin. It separated the blacks from the whites. You'd find all the blacks on this side and the majority of the whites on that side. There are very few blacks that live beyond Route 113 now. Many people believe that road was designed that way to separate us. I believe that, too.

A street that runs from the Town of Berlin over to Route 113 was also used to separate the whites from the blacks. It was first called Branch Street, and then the white folks came together in that area and had it renamed Maryland Avenue. Back in 1981 or 1982 during my 10-year term as President of the Worcester County NAACP, we fought and we had it changed back to Branch Street.

Corrupt election practices with regards to race are nothing new in this county. The earliest I remember Dad was voting when I was around eleven, maybe twelve years old. We used to go out to the barbershop right by where the dual highway is now. I'd hear men always talking about voting and everything else. I heard him talk about Roosevelt and others, but I know he voted for Harry Truman for President.

The white people in this area had a way of buying the votes of blacks. I can remember when the bribe was either $5.00 or a half pint of whiskey. They'd come to us and say, *"I want you to vote for..."* such and such thing. *"If you will, I'll give you $5.00."* They didn't realize that some of these men that drank liquor would take the liquor, and then wouldn't even go vote. It was the same with the $5.00. They'd take the money, but not vote.

For over 250 years, there had never been a black elected in Worcester County as a County Commissioner or anything else, not even for mayor. We've had two well-known black men run. One of them was my 10th grade math teacher named Oliver Williams. We called him Proctor. At that time, he was a citizen who sat on the Town Council. He ran for County Commissioner and didn't make it, even though we thought he would. Gabe Purnell, who's a younger guy than I am, ran and didn't make it. We had one out of Pocomoke named Honiss Cane who was very well-known. Honiss ran and didn't make it.

For almost two years, every meeting that the County Commissioners had that was open to the public, I was there. I was there gathering information and representing the county NAACP, because we wanted to change the election system. I was there learning how they operated and everything. At the same time I was learning, I was preparing to sue them. It was a two-fold thing.

Worcester County had at-large voting. There were five districts, but anyone across the county could vote for anyone in the at-large district. It was totally illegal and the county got away with it. We had people from Snow Hill who were part of the committee. All of them are dead now except Gabe Purnell, Fannie Birckhead who lived in Snow Hill, and myself. We were able to sue the county for its illegal voting system.

Worcester County got a lawyer out of Philadelphia, Mississippi to represent them. It's the most racist place they could have gone to represent the Town of Berlin. We had two lawyers who came to my house. One was named Chris Brown who taught law in Baltimore. Debbie Jeon was a very powerful woman with the ACLU. They called me one afternoon and wanted to come down to talk to me and the other members of the committee. We did and Ms. Jeon said she'd represent us. At that time, money was not discussed. So, we began to move. We outlined our strategy and followed it to a T.

We fought and fought, one lawsuit after the other. We went to the appellate court in Richmond, Virginia, and it supported us. The judges gave Worcester County the opportunity to set up another election system that would help us as black people, but they took that one down too. Worcester County Commissioners would not give in. This case went all the way to the Supreme Court. It was March when they announced that the Supreme Court failed to hear the case, because we did our homework and studied the situation. We got information through the Federal government that proved the election rules were totally illegal. We made history here in this county.

I remember right before I went to Detroit, Michigan for the 1989 NAACP convention. Just before I left, a newspaper reporter had been down to Mom and Dad's house questioning them about me, the NAACP, and what I was doing. Mom wouldn't answer them. That afternoon, I stopped by and Mom was telling me about what all they were doing, trying to get her to talk. Mom wasn't going to talk to them anyway. I finally got on the phone and I called the young lady who was in charge of the news team. I went down to her office and told her, "*Don't you ever go to my mother and father's. They don't want to talk. Don't you ever go down there again.*"

Two days before I left, somebody took a brick and threw it at Mom and Dad's front screen that faced the road. It hit the door. I talked to the Berlin Police Chief, who was concerned and went down there. Clem and I left for the convention. When they learned I was gone, a reporter tried to interview them again, but they didn't get anything. When I got back, I found out about it and threatened to sue them. I said, *"You were told to stay away from there."* They left them alone after that.

Dad never had a whole lot to say. He only talked when he had to. When I first got involved with the NAACP, I'd lead and speak at most of those press conferences. Later on or maybe the next day, I would go down to Mom and Dad's house.

Dad said, *"Junior, I saw you on television last night."*
"Huh?"
"Yeah, I saw you on there. You were telling them white folks something, weren't you?"
The next week would go along and Dad would say the same thing, *"Yeah, you telling them something, ain't you Junior?"*

Dad's friend Lemond Jones was married to mom's sister Annie. He gave me the nickname of Martin Luther King. One day, Uncle Lemond told my dad, *"Junior's just like Martin Luther King. He's got a whole lot of mouth."* Dad didn't answer him. Uncle Lemond could've said two wrong words, but Dad wasn't going to answer him back. No way.

Dad would have a smile on his face when he picked up the newspaper and saw my name, which was his name. He would read it all the way through and could tell you what it said. I think if Dad had lived a little while longer, he would probably be just like he was back then. He would be happy in his own way, but not doing much talking.

XIV

Making History

I had no intentions whatsoever to run for elected office in Worcester County, because I was the Vice-President for the State of Maryland NAACP. In October of that year, I would have been elected to State President, but there were numerous people throughout this county who wanted me to run for County Commissioner. So, I hummed and hawed, hummed and hawed. Finally, I called and told them I would run. Becoming a County Commissioner was a challenge and a learning experience.

On Election Day, I was at the Multipurpose Building on Flower Street. That's where they held the first election in the black district. The court told the county that there should be a polling place in the minority district. Before that, we voted uptown with the white folks at the school. Anyway, they set up in the Multipurpose Building in the black district and I won. When Mom got the news, her reaction was *"My goodness."*

When I ran the first time out here in the black district, my opponent was an incumbent. He was the President of the County Commissioners and a teacher at Stephen Decatur High School. I beat him 2 to 1. On Election Day, he came and patted me on the back, *"Jim, I didn't want to run but . . . "*. I surely asked him, *"Who put you up?"* Then, he told me who wanted him to run. I said, *"Well, you didn't have to run if you didn't want to."* He wished me good luck. It rained that day and he had made a pot of soup. His tent was right across from mine. All of us went over there to get soup. In the next election, he supported me.

When I was sworn into that office, I knew the operation of the County Commissioners' work. I was surprised when the chief county administrator, who worked hand-in-hand with us, came to me before the election of our President. He said, *"Jim, you might have to run for President."* I said, *"Jerry, I don't want that. I don't want to do it. It's time-consuming."*

I did not feel totally welcomed when I first went there, but that soon changed down through the months, and I began to gain a lot of support. Some tried to find ways of not letting me succeed. Some of them were forced to accept me after making me go before the Ethics Committee. Nobody else had to go, but I did. They said I had a conflict of interest, being elected County Commissioner and being a member of the NAACP.

They didn't know that I resigned before I even started running, so they carried it before the ethics committee. The meeting didn't last ten minutes. They ruled in my favor when they learned

I was no longer involved with the NAACP. I wasn't even Vice-President or anything.

They did everything they could to try and stop me, but I held that office for twenty years. It took 253 years, but I was the first black ever to become Commissioner in Worcester County. I was also the first black chosen to serve as their Vice-President, which I did for 12 years. I led the County Commissioners as President for two years.

My bill from the attorneys that represented us during the illegal voting lawsuit was $378,000. I was elected as a County Commissioner before the bill came out. I was in a meeting when it came across our desk. A lot of people were worried that I'd have to pay it. The county had to pay not only my attorneys, but also about $600,000 to their attorney. In essence, Worcester County spent almost a million dollars to keep from electing a black County Commissioner. That's how bad it was back then.

I came onboard new, but I had a lot of firepower in me then and I wouldn't back down from nothing. I did it in a nice quiet way. I didn't use profane language then or now, but I would raise my voice every now and then, if needed. Some Commissioners were hard-nosed, like the ones who own Trimper's Rides in Ocean City, and own the Chevrolet place in Berlin. They wanted to be known as the ones who run Worcester County. I wouldn't let them do it.

The man over at the Chevrolet place, Jim Barrett, called me not long after I got elected. They were getting ready to elect officers for the County Commissioners. He said, *"Jim, I'm running for President. I want you to vote for me."*

I stopped Barrett in his tracks. I said, *"Jim, I might want to run,"* knowing I wasn't going to run, even though I had been asked by the Administrator. I said, *"Jim, don't you ever call this house again to tell me who to vote for, or how to vote."*

"And we got a loaning bill we want to get through and I want you to support that." I said, *"Don't you call me about that. I make my own decisions. I might make them before I leave here, and I might make them when I get to the meeting room. That's why I never tell you what's on my mind. I make my own decisions, then you'll know."*

Jim Barrett didn't call me anymore. He was one of those that tried to keep this landfill open. He told me he was fighting the people to keep it open, but told the people he wanted it closed. I went up to D.C., and he stood up in front of the place. I said, *"Why are you here Jim? You told me you wanted to get a consent order to keep it open."* The lady said, *"What?"*

I showed him up right in that committee meeting. His face was just as red. He said, *"I did not tell you that."* I said, *"You told me in my yard the day before that you were coming up here to try to keep it open."* A man named Icebaum said, *"Mr. Purnell, he lied to you."* I never will forget it. Jim Barrett never did bother me after that.

Four years went by. When it was time for the next election, the polling place was moved over to the school, but few blacks live over there. I challenged it somewhat and then backed off. A white man ran against me and I beat him 3 to 1. We always thought that one of the reasons they moved that polling place out of the black district over to a white district was to cause my defeat sooner or later. From then on, whoever ran against me, I always beat them 2 to 1 or 3 to 1.

One of the biggest thing I learned being in that office is that this county was not quite ready for a black County Commissioner. Initially the others tried to maneuver themselves around me. If we were in a meeting talking about an issue, rezoning or whatever, it would require a vote. We'd discuss it before we voted. For a while, my statements went on deaf ears, but I'm the type of person who stands my ground.

I did not run my mouth all the time. I sat back and I listened. There were times they would discuss an issue and I wouldn't say a word. Not one word. If that issue went on, and on, and on, I would be the one to stop it, and I'd tell them the reason why. I would throw it to a vote. When I first got in there, if I called a vote, they'd ignore it. Eventually, that changed. I could put in a motion and get it seconded. Nine times out of ten, I'd get it approved. So, it took a while.

When I decided not to run again, they labeled me the smartest County Commissioner that had ever been there. I didn't expect them to say that. They didn't say it to me privately. In a public meeting on my last day in office, the President of the County Commissioners said, *"Here is the smartest Commissioner that has ever been in this office."* It was also said by a lot of businesspeople associated with the Board and by others associated with the operation of county government.

I didn't look for glory or great recognition or anything. I just went on about my business. I hadn't paid much attention to it, but I have been told that a lot of blacks have positions inside the government office building than before. They said they'd walked in and out of there back then, and it was lily-white. Walk in there now, there's a lot of blacks there.

Before I got elected, we had a black warden. He retired and his assistant Garry Mumford was in line for the job. They tried to stop him because he was dating the warden's daughter and eventually married her. What does that have to do with him being appointed or hired as a warden of the jail? We live in the United States of America. That's a far crimination.

I said to one of the female County Commissioners, who was against it, *"You mean to tell me that you won't support him because he's going with the warden's daughter? Why?"* "Well, he might get ideas from what his father-in-law tells him." I said, "Nah, it doesn't work that way." I made a statement that if he didn't get that job, I was gonna have the television stations, newspapers, and everything out here. By that time, the newspapers followed me where I went anyway. When the deal went down, he got the job and it was a unanimous vote.

When the Commissioners got ready to discuss his salary, they wanted to curtail it. They wanted to pay him on a trial basis. I said, *"Well, he's been assistant warden now for Lord knows how many years."* After the first year, he got the $115,000 salary he deserved.

Garry Mumford passed away a few months ago. He was fifty-seven years old. I went to his funeral at Holloway Hall on the Salisbury State University campus. More than a thousand people attended and that place couldn't hold everyone. I listened to them talk about him and his work. A lot of things ran through my mind about what he went through. I wondered if I, or someone like me, hadn't been there, would he have gotten that job? If that Commission had been all white, he may not have.

Of all the county department heads, whether it be the Sheriff or Administrators, we only had one that's black and that was Garry Mumford. He came and thanked me many a day. He was a very strong supporter in my campaign too. He, his father, his wife, and other people joined hands. I didn't have to do a lot of campaigning myself. They did it for me, which was a blessing, because I didn't get out in the street to walk door to door. I don't walk that much, so I accepted every little bit of help I could get. They came to my rescue.

I cherish all my brothers and sisters, living or dead, because when I was out here running for office, they all supported me in a mighty way. Encouragement was one of the things that meant more to me than money. They encouraged me to go on. Then on top of that, they would acknowledge the goodness that I had done and thank me. My brothers and sisters mean everything to me and they still do.

I continued to run for County Commissioner until I got tired and decided it was time to give it up. I didn't want to stay in office forever and ever and ever. The people periodically need a dose of someone else to come with different ideas. Nine times out of ten, they're good ideas that help benefit the county. It was time for some new blood to come in all the way across the board, and they got some of it. When I retired, so did some of my key supporters. When the news finally came out that I was not running, there were a lot of black and white people who asked me if I would think about continuing, even down to the school board. I thought it over and made my mind up. I made my remarks that I wasn't going to run anymore, and they said, *"You know you'll get elected."* I said, *"That's why I'm not gonna run no more."* With that kind of mindset, people get very complacent. It was time for a change.

There's a lady that lives down the road from me named Diane Purnell. She's somewhat younger than I am. I got behind her and supported her when she ran. Diane won and is doing a great job. She's got one more year left on her four-year term, and then she'll be up for reelection if she chooses to run.

I have often said that I've been blessed. I've had the opportunity to help make a difference for all of the kids in this county and for the county in general. When I first got elected County Commissioner, I was asked by one of the newspapers, *"Now that you're elected, what do you expect to accomplish?"* My response was, *"If I can arrange it so that the people on the other side of the aisle, who happen to be white, and us as black people can come together at the table, talk about our differences, work through our differences, and help make a change in those differences for better, then I think we've accomplished a lot."*

I've been asked numerous times, did that ever take place? Yes, it did. I've seen it. I've met with a lot of Maryland leaders, from this county and others. There's a difference in state hiring practices across the board. That probably wouldn't have happened if I, or someone like me, hadn't been elected. So, that has changed. With the help of black people in this county, we've accomplished quite a bit. There's always room for more. Each day as we go along, we should be helping to make a change somewhere and somehow, so that our kids and people in this county can see a difference. I think we're starting to come up to where we want it to be.

XV

Stagnant Progress in Our Schools

When you talk to kids nowadays about racism, they look at you with a strange lack of understanding. They don't know it firsthand. As black leaders in this county and others, we began to get on the school boards and tell them they must have black history instruction in the classroom, so the kids know the importance of George Washington Carver, Eli Whitney, Booker T. Washington, and down the line. That bothered and continues to bother some white folks because they want everyone to believe they explored and created everything.

The hiring of black teachers and principals in this county school system is a shame. When I first became President of the Worcester County NAACP, we were struggling and working with the Board of Education. It was a five-member, appointed school board then. Once they were elected by district, it became a seven-member school board. There were two blacks on it. We would challenge the Board on hiring black teachers. The excuse was there were none. Why not? They attend school, graduate, go to college, and graduate with a teaching degree. The Board would not hire them.

The year after I was elected, the county was working on their budget. We concluded on money for the hiring of the teachers, the sheriff's department money, and all. That's how we pay their salaries.

They came and asked me to support the budget. I turned around, looked at them sternly, and said, *"What'd you say?"* *"Will you support us in this year's budget?"* I told the Superintendent of Schools, *"I will not and I shall not vote in favor of this Board of Education budget, not until there are some blacks teachers hired. I don't mean one, two, or three . . . SOME black teachers are hired in this system. Taxation without representation is wrong. We're paying taxes, but we're not being represented in places where we should be. So, I will not, and I will encourage my people that I come in contact with in this county not to support the budget."*

That year they hired fourteen black teachers. The year before, they didn't hire one. The next year, I think they ended up hiring about six. I'm not saying it's because of me, but it happened during the administration I was a part of. For the last five years or so, I doubt this Board of Education has hired five black teachers. Stephen Decatur High School, the largest high school by student population on this side of the Bay Bridge, has no black teachers.

It had a black teacher named Leona Mack who started here in her twenties. She would be in Future Business Leaders of America, the FBLA, and she took her classes up to Hagerstown, and all the conferences. I guess she stayed there about thirty years until she got sick with diabetes, and eventually retired. Before she could get out that door, they hired a young white guy to replace her. They should have waited until after school had closed to advertise that job, because that's the proper process. All I know, this young man was walking around the school and nothing else. He wasn't prepared, but they hired him.

There is one black Vice-Principal. The Vice-Principal she replaced was black. It's sad when you look at the number of African-American kids at Stephen Decatur, and no one looks like them. They have no black teachers to look up to. These white teachers can and do tell these black kids anything. Then once these teachers are challenged on it, they want to pass the buck back to the parents, because *"the parents didn't do this"* and *"the parents didn't do that."* The parents don't hire the teachers. The Board of Education does. That's part of the problem.

This school does a poor job of acknowledging the accomplishments of its black students. There's a girl who just graduated and she's going to Harvard. She's got a four-year, full ride scholarship. No one just walks into Harvard any kind of way. Come Awards Night at the school, nobody knew about it. The only way it got out was because the award she received came from an outside organization. She's a great track runner. Her final ride on my bus as a high school student was up to Morgan State for a meet. No one would ever know she's on the bus. She's small in stature and a very brilliant, bright girl. No one in the school system or on Board of Education even acknowledged her or the award that she received.

Stephen Decatur also had a star football player named Benny Tate. That school failed to acknowledge his accomplishments, showcase his talents, or help him connect with various college football programs throughout this country. So, his father withdrew him from Stephen Decatur and enrolled him in Snow Hill High School. The student population there is about three-fourths black. They have some black teachers. The Vice-Principal was black, and now their Principal is black.

Down at Snow Hill, them folks got what they wanted and needed. The whole school began to showcase Benny Tate and got with ESPN. He went places. He attended Auburn University on scholarship and was drafted by the Houston Texans in the second round. That brought him a little bit of money.

When white girls and boys achieve academically or athletically, the school makes sure that everyone know about it. That's not the case with black students. Two others, a boy and a girl, were acknowledged the other night for high marks. I don't know how much money they received. My sister Bert's grandson received well over $5,000 worth of money and grants during Awards Night. He's going to UMES over in Princess Anne. However, of all the money that was distributed to the honorees, there were only about five to seven black students. Something's wrong with that picture. At Awards Night, one speaker said, *"I feel hurt because I don't see as many African-Americans up here that should be."*

The teachers are in charge of that ceremony and decide which students get recognized. When the kids walked across that stage at graduation, we saw how few blacks got any sort of financial support. We got a basketball player who graduated and got a full ride to a college down south which is well-known for its basketball program. He ended up getting a scholarship he didn't even know he was going to get. Those white kids got scholarships of $40,000 or $50,000. Blacks got $600 or $700. That's unbelievable. Blacks walked out with not even enough to get a spoonful of Corn Flakes.

All the system is doing is overlooking them and leaving them out there in the back row. That needs to stop. I'm afraid that this education system we have now is to the point that our kids will not be able to survive. I see it coming. I talk about it to people who are in power. We wonder why certain things happen in this education system that should not. The people that are in charge let them get away with it. When a superintendent of a school system allows certain things to happen, then he's at fault.

He should be called on the carpet and chastised for those things that happened under his administration.

We look back as blacks at our education leaders, who are white and are less likely to care about our children's education. It's bad. A lot of that's happening today, right here in this county and across the state of Maryland. As I've traveled, I heard a story in New Orleans. The man was talking about his Board of Education and how corrupt it is. I thought we only had that here in Worcester County, but it's countrywide. I just finished talking with black teachers and dealing and the hiring of black teachers countrywide. I don't know if any good will come out of it or not. I hope so. In the long run, I don't know if I'll be around to see it.

XVI

The Downfall is Coming

The election of last year showed us how society seems to be changing and, at the same time, how it hasn't. I was shocked to find out the Republican nominee for President was invited to this high school. It was an even bigger shock when I found out it was reality. When he came here, I happened to be on the road around Cambridge. Clem called and told me they brought him down Flower Street. He didn't go down a major highway. He came down through the black neighborhood.

The guy that organized it graduated from Stephen Decatur some years ago and was one of his workers. When I looked at television that night and saw who was standing on the stage, one of them is my Supervisor of Transportation and the other was the Superintendent of Schools. One of the principals from that school, some from other schools, plus a few other people I know were on that stage. They no doubt bought into his agenda.

He's going to challenge the Voting Rights Act and if he gets support, he'll do away with it. If he can get around the Constitution, he's going to do it. He will carry us backward and that's not good. I get upset when I see black people supporting him. It makes me wonder why they do it and where their heads are. They're somewhat weak-minded. If they go back and look at where they came from, what they came through, how they got here, and then listen to him, then they'll find out what his intentions are. They're not good for us.

I was even upset when I saw Ben Carson, although he's a Republican. When they first started campaigning, he was leading. When he started losing ground, the eventual nominee began to talk about Carson like a dog, yet he's sitting on his team now. That's scary. He has no principles.

There was no substance in his platform speeches to even make me think about taking him seriously. I can't take him seriously. With all that's going on with the current occupant of the White House, if they don't soon put a muzzle on him, all of America will be looking like fools. That's why some of the Republicans are beginning to back off of him and not support his agenda. I am quite sure before it's all over with, some of his black supporters will be ashamed of themselves and want to go hide.

I feel he's doing more harm to this country and our international standing than good, because he's embarrassing. He doesn't mind embarrassing others. He'll do it and think nothing of it. He doesn't get embarrassed, because he doesn't have enough sense to get embarrassed.

I was on a bus trip to Philadelphia recently and was talking to a couple of bus drivers. We were in a hospitality room they had fixed up for us, eating and watching television until it's time to go back home. I said, *"It wouldn't surprise me if he doesn't end up like Richard Nixon." "What you mean, Jim?" "Resigning from office or impeached."* That's where he's headed. He's leaving himself open for impeachment. It's going to take a while, but I think some of them Republicans are out to get him now.

There's an election coming up next year for some of those in Congress and state legislatures. They cannot afford to support him with all this mess he has out here, and expect to get reelected. If they do, someone's going to be taking their place. They have to take a hard look at themselves and decide whether they're going to continue their support. Most of them who have good sense will not. At least that's the way I hope.

This country is nowhere like it used to be. We're not as safe as we may think we are, messing with North Korea. We need to leave them alone. They're not bothering us. Keep fooling with North Korea and the next thing you know, they'll send a bomb over here. I think this thing about the Russians being involved in that election will be his downfall, and he knows it too. We'll see.

XVII

Advice

We cannot sit idly by and let everything that our ancestors struggled and died for slip away. We should not act like everything's okay when it's not. I got on some people about that recently. We've become too complacent. That's what wrong with the civil rights movement today - complacency. We got out here and fought alongside Dr. King and others. We talked about the dream, but now that's he's gone I think those so-called dreamers stopped dreaming. We think that we have arrived. We think that we've reached the mountaintop. We stopped getting involved in trying to make a difference. Some thought that everything was A-Okay, but it wasn't.

People can see what is happening right now. The undercover racists are coming out the woodwork. They want to do away with the Voting Rights Act. That was our protection. Anything that was productive for Afro-Americans, they want to get their hands on and do away with it. There are so few of us who can combat that and I'm so afraid it might go away.

I was talking to a group down at the Snow Hill Library a few weeks ago. I told them then, I take this seriously, because all that work should not go in vain. There's a lot of challenges out here now when we get the door closed in our face, and then we wonder why. If we would stop to think that if we just kept getting involved, maybe when they got ready to close that door we could put our foot in to stop it. They'll know why we stopped it. I'm so afraid it's going to be a steep uphill struggle. I can say that because I've been involved in a lot of stuff that has taken place here in this county up to this very moment.

I've seen a lot of name-calling. That has been done to black people since we've been here, but we overlooked that and moved on. However, we do not want to become undignified. We do not want to lower ourselves to their level. Let them go ahead and say what they have to say. However, don't turn around and get yourself caught up in that web so that you're as bad off as they are.

In the current education system, parent involvement is necessary. Parents need to take the reins and advocate for their children, not just academically, but socially. Parents have got to do their share of the work in order for this whole dynamic machine to come together and work well for all sides. If that doesn't happen with black parents, it never will happen for black children. Kids come home from school with homework. A lot of the black kids will go back out in the street, play until the sun goes down, and then their parents make them go in the house. Instead of them doing homework, what do you think they do? They go to bed. No homework is done. That's a big setback for those kids. Parents have got their work cut out for them, but they need to make sure their kids at least do that minimum.

Parents need to encourage the next generation of dreamers. When I have the opportunity, I've always tell them that they need to get behind their children. Don't let that Board of Education tell them they're not capable of certain subjects. We've had situations here where kids were signed up for a subject like Algebra I. That teacher came back and told them, *"You can't do Algebra I"*. If that child and his mother or father decide that he or she should take it, why should those teachers or teacher assistants control that child's course of study? The teachers took that class at some point. Why can't the kids if they feel they're ready? They've got to stop letting others dictate to them, whether it's teachers or their friends. That's what's happened to these kids now. Without that academic growth, these kids are limiting their options. They will find themselves out there alone and not knowing which way to turn. Because of the people I see getting involved, this system can turn around.

We cannot depend on the elderly people to do our job for us. If we want something done for our children, we need to get out there and get involved ourselves. We can't afford to sit around and depend on Joe Blow to do this for us or do that for us. We can't do that. We need to get out there, get involved, and let our children know that we're supporting them for the right reasons. When that happens, we'll see that these kids will make a difference. Most of the kids in school today want to be there.

If a child opens his or her mind and believes *"I am going to do this"* or *"I am going to do that"*, as long as it's in the right way, let him or her do it. Don't let anyone say he can't do it or she should not do it. Don't let anybody tell them that. If they've got it in their hearts to do it, then encourage them. Nine times out of ten, it'll turn out right.

Even those of us who don't have children of our own can offer guidance or a word of encouragement to keep the kids in our community on the right track. We've got some brave black kids coming out of here now. We've always had them, but now they've got a chance to go farther than we ever thought we could.

List of Image Sources

(All images provided by family unless otherwise noted)

Photo of James L. Purnell Jr. in 4th grade, Berlin, MD, circa 1945.

Photo of the Germantown School yard on Flower Street, Berlin, MD, date unknown.

Obituary of Minnie Jarman, The Daily Times (Salisbury, MD), Volume 29, Dec. 12, 1952

Photo of the Purnell Family in Berlin, MD, 1961. Seated - James Sr. and Hulda; Standing – Osie Henry, James L. Purnell Jr., Patricia Purnell Hingleton, Gerald Purnell Sr., Benjamin H. Purnell Sr., Hennie Purnell Chase, Bertha C. Purnell.

Ad for Sunshine Laundry, The Daily Times (Salisbury, MD), Volume 30, No. 36, Nov. 30, 1953, p.7

Photo of Alice M. McCray and John Brittingham in Berlin, MD, 1940s.

Photo of Harvey A. Tyre, taken in Philadelphia, PA, date unknown.

Photo of John E. McCray and Sallie Bertha Tyre McCray, location unknown, 1940s.

Photo of Eben H. Tyre, taken at Frankford Camp, Antioch A.M.E. Church, Frankford, DE, date unknown.

Photo of Rayne's Reef, Berlin, MD, 1979. The Maryland Historical Trust, Maryland Inventory of Historic Properties, WO-167, photo 57.

Photo of the Globe Theater, Berlin, MD, date unknown.

Photo of the Henry Hotel, Ocean City, MD, date unknown.

Photo of newly captured German sailors from U-858 submarine, Cape Henlopen, DE, date unknown. Delaware Public Archives, Delaware in the World War II Collection, RG 1325.206 Delaware in World War II, Record Identifier 852.

Index

A&P Grocery Store 21, 51
AAU Basketball 77-78
ACLU 83
Acme Poultry 15
Annapolis (MD) 33
Asheville (NC) 77
Atlantic General Hospital 28
Bahamas 61
Ball Theater 36
Baltimore (MD) 80
Barrett, Jim 90-91
Baseball 27-28, 61
Beckett, Alex 8, 36, 40; Ben 36; Bill 8, 42; Emma "Lib" McCray 37, 42; George 36;
Berlin (MD) 1, 12, 15, 27, 36, 49-52, 61, 65, 80-81, 83, 85, 89
Berlin Milling Company 9, 23, 28, 31, 33, 44
Berlin Eagles 27
Best, Bill 16
Birckhead, Fannie 83
Black Hills 77
Board of County Commissioners 82-83, 87, 89-93, 95, 97
Board of Education 13, 71, 97-100, 102, 109
Board of Health 24, 80
Bohemians 61
Boston (MA) 68
Boy Scouts 5
Bowie State College 37
Branch Street 53, 81;
Briddell, Jess 58; John 16
Briddelltown 1, 55-59, 61

Briddelltown Improvement Committee 79-80
Bridgeton (NJ) 27
Brittingham, Alice McCray 1, 31, 33-34, 37, 40, 42, 57; John 31-34
Brown, Chris 83
Buckingham High School 27
Burbage Funeral Home 5
bus transportation 10, 71-78
butter production and sales 20-21
Calloway, Cab 65
campaign 87-88, 91, 94
Cane, Honiss 82
Carson, Ben 104
Carver, George Washington 13, 97
Casino 62
Chevrolet 62, 89-90
chores 18-20, 22
Clayton Theater 36
Coard, Upshur 72
Coastal Furnishings 67-68
Colored Excursions 65
complacency 107-110
crabbing 63
Crownsville (MD) 33-34
Davis, Ralph 28
death rattles 39-40
Delaware Day 66
Dennis, Bob 11; Helen 71
Derrickson, Henry 16
Detroit (MI) 84
Donaway Furniture 51
drapery installation business 67-70
Eagle Poultry 36

Ellington, Duke 65
entertainment 27-28, 53-54, 61, 63
family 1-11, 14-28, 30-52, 55, 61-62, 71, 79, 85, 94
financial aid 99-101
Flower Street 1, 8-9, 11, 16, 23, 26-27, 34, 54-55, 85, 103
food preparation 2, 15-21, 47
Foster, Joe 16
Frankord (DE) 41
Frankford Camp 7-8, 35-36
Future Business Leaders of America 98
German measles 62
German prisoners 36, 61-63
Germantown Road 72
Germany 62-63
Glasssboro (NJ) 31
Globe Theater 53-54
Grand Terrace Dance Hall 65
Gray, Arthur 46; Ella 45; Lizzie 45; Margaret/Madge 45;
Great Depression 44
grief 7
Hagerstown (MD) 98
Haney, Britt 71
Harrison Hall 66
Harrison's 9, 31, 61
Hazelton (PA) 68
Henry, Dameion 69; Delores 31; Elkie 37; Ernest 10; Louise 55;
Henry Hotel 55-56
High Point (NC) 72-73
hiring practices 97-99
hog killing 15-16
Hood, Goldie 59
Hudson, Dave 57-59; Martha 57; Noah "Nowie" 51-52;

Tommy 43; Victoria Purnell 6, 43; Vivian 6, 18;
ice skating 55
Icebaum, Mr. 91
illness 3-4, 7, 22, 39
Jacobs, Bertha McCray 38-40
Jarman, Ike 58; Minnie 11-12
Jeon, Debbie 83
Joe Holland Shoe Store 51
Johnson, Charlie 59; Eddie 59; Tommy 59
Jones, Anna 37, 85; Lemond 85
King, Martin Luther 14, 78, 81, 85, 107
Knight, Carlton 20; Jean 19-20; Shirley 20
Labor Day 65-66
landfill 8, 79-81, 90
Laurel (MD) 67
Lorraine Hotel 78
Long Island (NY) 68
Mack, Leona 98
Madison Square Garden 77
Maryland Avenue 53, 81;
Maryland Day 66
May Day 34
McCabe, Joshua 56-57; Morris 9
McCray, John 7, 35-38, 40; Joshua "Jock" 3, 7, 38-41; Sallie Bertha Tyre 35, 37-40
Memphis (TN) 77
migrant camps 19, 26, 54
milk production and sales 17-20, 22, 24-26, 52
Millsboro (DE) 38-39
Millsboro Dairy 36
Morgantown (WV) 77
movie theaters 36, 53
Mumford, Garry 92-94

NAACP 80, 83-85, 87-89, 97
Nelson, Ben 71
New York City (NY) 77
Newark (MD) 12-13
Nichols/Nickels, Dr. 3
North Carolina 19, 54
North Korea 105
Ocean City (MD) 55, 65, 67-69, 74, 79, 89
orchards 9
Peninsula General Hospital 23, 28
Pennywell, Gene 69
Philadelphia (MS) 83
Philadelphia (PA) 4-5, 40, 45, 105
Philadelphia Apex School 6
Phillips Canning Company 62
Pitts, Ari 5; Ella Mae Purnell 5-6, 16-17
Pocomoke 12, 36, 71, 75, 82
police 5, 50-52, 54, 85
police brutality 51-52
possum (as food) 47
prisoners of war 61-63
Purnell, Anthony 69; Benjamin 3-4, 30; Bertha "Bert" 3-4; Clara 46, 48; Clem 77-78, 103; Diane 95; Edward 3-4, 7; Elwood 10, 15, 23, 31, 33, 44, 46, 52; Gabe 79, 82; Gerald Sr. 3-4, 7, 18, 21; Gerald Jr. 69; Gilbert 3-7; Hattie 16-17; Hennie 3-5, 45, 55; Hennie Mary Gray 43-48; Hulda "Hilda" McCray 1-5, 7-9, 11, 17, 20-222, 24, 27, 31, 34-35, 37-40, 42, 45-46, 48, 51, 55, 57, 59, 62, 79, 84, 85; James Lee Sr. 1-9, 11, 15-27, 31, 33, 35, 39, 44-48, 50-52, 56-57, 59, 61-62, 79; Lee 23, 43-44, 47-48, 52, 58; Oliver 27, 71-72; Patricia "Tisch" 3, 6-7, 11, 22, 51-52, 62; Terrence 69; Virginia 3, 6-7; Winifred 4, 46, 48;
Purnell Dairy Farm 1, 15-22, 24-26, 52

quarantine 62
Quillen, Mr. 23
rabbits (as food) 21, 43, 47
racetrack 62
racism 13, 49-56, 65, 81, 97
Rayne's 49-50
Red Ryder and Little Beaver comic books 8
Red Star Bus Lines 49
retaliation 53-54, 56
Richmond (VA) 84
Robertson, Dr. 22
ROTC 77
Russia 105
Saint Paul U.M. Church 21
Salisbury (MD) 67
Salley, Dr. 21
school 8-13, 34-35, 37, 41, 55, 61-62, 97
school bus contracting 71-78
Scott, Howard 27
Seahawk Road 55, 61
segregation, bathroom 49; Halloween parade 52-53; in the Atlantic Ocean 66; movie theater 53-54; on the beach and boardwalk 65-66; on the streets 49- 54, 81; restaurant 49-50, 54;
Shockley, Dollie 40; Elmer (Chief) 52
Showell, Bashie 37
Smyrna (DE) 41
Smoky Mountains 77
Snow Hill (MD) 12, 27, 36, 72, 83
Snow Hill High School 100
Somerset County 61
squirrel (as food) 47
Steele, Johnny 38

students 76-77
Sunshine Laundry 28-30
Supreme Court 84
Tampa (FL) 19-20
Tate, Benny 100
Temple University Hospital 4-5
Truman, Harry (President) 82
Tyre, Cyrus 38; Eben 41-42; Harvey 35;
Udell, Jack 36
U.S. President (45th) 103-105
vandalism 85
Virginia Day 66
vocational training 67-68
Von Davis Tractors 51
voting 82-83, 89
Voting Rights Act 103, 107
Washington (D.C.) 68, 80
Washington, Booker T. 97
water contamination 80
water hole 55
Waters, Zula 71
Whirlpool Corporation 67
Whitney, Eli 97
Willards (MD) 17
Williams, Oliver 82
World War II 31-32
Worcester High School 12-14

www.ingramcontent.com/pod-product-compliance
Lightning Source LLC
Chambersburg PA
CBHW032054150426
43194CB00006B/526